CHEERING FOR THE GOOD:
Leading When It Matters

KAREN LUECK

outskirts
press

Cheering for the Good: Leading When It Matters
All Rights Reserved.
Copyright © 2021 Karen Lueck
v4.0

The opinions expressed in this manuscript are solely the opinions of the author and do not represent the opinions or thoughts of the publisher. The author has represented and warranted full ownership and/or legal right to publish all the materials in this book.

This book may not be reproduced, transmitted, or stored in whole or in part by any means, including graphic, electronic, or mechanical without the express written consent of the publisher except in the case of brief quotations embodied in critical articles and reviews.

Outskirts Press, Inc.
http://www.outskirtspress.com

ISBN: 978-1-9772-3272-4

Cover Photo © 2021 www.gettyimages.com. All rights reserved - used with permission.

Outskirts Press and the "OP" logo are trademarks belonging to Outskirts Press, Inc.

PRINTED IN THE UNITED STATES OF AMERICA

TABLE OF CONTENTS

Note to Reader i
Introduction iii
1. Leading as Everyone's Call 1
2. Focusing the Energy of the Spirit 12
3. Reclaiming Goodness 20
4. Searching for Meaning and Purpose 29
5. Believing in Our Oneness 37
6. Embracing Vulnerability 46
7. Claiming Our Voice 55
8. Seeing Into Being 64
9. Using Power to Make a Difference 71
10. Communicating the Mission 79
11. Working Collaboratively 89
12. Motivating Movement Through Questions 97
13. Moving Through Fear and Loss 104
14. Developing My Inner Cheer Leader 111
15. Standing on Holy Ground 118
Glossary 121
Bibliography 123
Acknowledgements 128

NOTE TO READER

I finished the writing of this book just as COVID-19 was spreading from Asia to Europe. As I re-read the text to see if it would still be relevant in a post-COVID world, I realized that what it contains is more relevant now than ever. What I proposed in the book as the kind of leadership we need today actually played out during the crisis as people stepped forward to contribute their gifts, to cheer others on, and to work for the common good. I inserted some of these inspiring examples in the text, but left the rest intact.

In the post-COVID world, we will need to decide together as a people and as a planet who we are now. We will need resources to reflect on where we are and where we want to be in the future. May this book become for you an instrument of reflection and a catalyst to create a new and even better world with and for others.

It has been my honor to be here for you in this way. Continue cheering for the good.

Love,
Karen

"I have set before you life and death, blessings and curses. Choose life so that you and your descendants may live."

(Deuteronomy 30: 19 NRSV)

INTRODUCTION

The score is tied. There are two minutes left in this hard-fought basketball game, and our star player has just fouled out. Throughout the game, there have been some questionable calls by the refs, and fans on both sides are angry. It's hot in the gym, and people are red-faced and sweating. Stress and anxiety are etched on everyone's face. The game is on the line. We are on the sidelines. WHAT DO WE DO??

The family is gathering for the holiday with members on both sides of the bitter partisan political divide. Each side begins to yell louder, trying to prove the rightness of their ideology and the idiocy and downright dangerousness of the other. Relationships, once very close, are fracturing. Everyone's face is contorted with anger, fear, or pain. The family is on the line. We are on the sidelines. WHAT DO WE DO??

The earth is rapidly warming, with the resultant increase in extreme weather events, rising sea levels, and species extinction. Waves of people are migrating in order to survive. Pandemics are spreading worldwide. Wealthy corporations are putting greed over service to the whole. The most vulnerable in our midst are being targeted as scapegoats. People are unsettled; anxiety and fear are ramping up. The life of the planet is on the line. We are on the sidelines. WHAT DO WE DO??

In times of great change and turmoil like these, people often feel helpless, hopeless, and afraid. They don't know what to do to make things better. Because they don't trust themselves and their neighbors enough, too often, unfortunately, they cede their power and look to a strong leader to save them. They want the leader to show his/her power with a war-like stance, where there's no room for compromise, where there's only one correct way, and where everyone blindly agrees with the so-called leader.

Does this sound familiar? It is what many people in the world are experiencing right now. Our own country has been split into camps, yelling at each other and blaming each other rather than figuring out how to work together. And leaders have been known to exacerbate the problem by saying, "Trust me. I am the only one who can save you." We don't need more individualistic and divisive rhetoric. So, WHAT DO WE DO??

We need to step up! All of us. We must look at "leadership" differently. We need to return to the concept of a leader as one who focuses on the common good rather than on his/her own needs, recognizes the goodness and the strength of the people rather than what's wrong with them, inspires us to be our better selves. The models of leadership we need today call for much more collaboration, compassion, inclusion, humility, and emotional intelligence. Especially in these painful and desperate times, we need leaders who cheer us on, proclaiming that together we can make the world a better place.

And that's what we've seen lately. Many leaders have come to the fore during the COVID 19 crisis. They have put the common good ahead of their own comfort and safety at times. They have spread the message that we are all in this together and that we must look out for everyone. They have used their creativity to serve the needs of the whole. When the COVID 19 pandemic is behind us, we will need to make decisions about who we want to be as a people. Will we go back to who we were before, or will this challenging time have been a point of transformation for all of us?

Hopefully, each of us will continue to step up like we did during this crisis. There are many kinds of leaders – commanders, teachers, experts, gurus, and others – and each is needed in different types of situations. But because of our present situation in the world, where all seems to be chaos and people feel helpless, I think we need to emphasize a leadership style which encourages and facilitates each of us to engage our own leadership potential, which says "Let's do this together." Therefore, my focus in this book will be on the type of leaders I call *cheer leaders*.

I was a cheerleader in high school. (Go, St. Boniface New Hawks!) I was part of a team who corralled the energy in the gym into a positive force for good. Since then, as I engaged in various ministries throughout my life, I found myself continuing to look for the potential for good in my students or clients. Instead of focusing on diagnoses or deficits in people, I found myself recognizing and encouraging their strength and gifts. Early on, in my doctoral thesis entitled "And She Was Very Good," I proposed a new methodology for pastoral counselors to focus on empowering the client's goodness and strengths rather than on fixing what is perceived to be wrong with him/her. When I started writing inspirational articles, I usually based them on a good that showed up in my life that day, whether that be an inspiring person, a turtle who had appeared in my path, or the moon illuminating the night.

Looking back on all this, what I realized recently is that I never really stopped acting like a cheerleader. I still look for the good; I still cheer people on. But now I am a *cheer leader*, one who cheers in a larger arena than a gym. Now I cheer for humanity and for all of creation. It's not just a game for which we're cheering, it's our life. So, to signal this distinction throughout the book, when I refer to a school's team-based cheerleading, I will use the compound word "cheerleader." When I refer to the call to all of us at this time, to step up and encourage others, I will use the term *"cheer leader."*

Recently, I finished a four-year term as the president of my religious community, the Franciscan Sisters of Perpetual Adoration (FSPA), based in La Crosse, Wisconsin. This role, along with my previous ministries, has given me experience in recognizing what effective leadership looks like in the 21st century, and what it doesn't. But it has been now when I'm no longer in an official leadership position that I've been finding out more deeply why all of us need to step up as leaders. I still feel an urgency to make things better in the world, but now I no longer have an official title or platform from which to do it. The question for me is this – how to continue to influence through positive leadership? I needed to go outside my comfort zone and recognize where my gifts might be needed at this time.

One way I found to do this was to become an author. This time it's in an even larger arena, where I risk putting my words and ideas in print and facing failure or negative pushback. It's an emotionally and psychically challenging process, but God continues to call. Each morning I awake with renewed energy and enthusiasm for the task, so excited about partnering with my readers in making the world a better place. In addition,

I volunteer at some non-profits and serve on several boards and committees where I can continue to influence for the good. In all these ways I rub elbows with like-minded people who care deeply about humanity and all of creation.

At the same time, I continue to be an ordinary person like you who has unique quirks and hidden potential. I love changing things up all the time, which is great, but I have a hard time with the mundane details involved in change. I love team games, but I crave solitude. I can see the big picture, but find myself nesting at home. I love mystery, but want a happy ending. Underneath it all, I search for meaning and purpose. And part of that meaning is to share my gifts with others. So, here I am. And you can be, too, with your own gifts, environment, and networks.

You will find that God, Christianity, and my Catholic faith are very important to me, and underpin everything I do as a person and as a leader. One of my core beliefs is that we are all created basically good and remain basically good. This belief is referred to as "the Catholic principle" (even though popular preaching through the years has not always embraced this concept very well.) Even when we sin, the spark of the Divine remains central to our being. This is who I am and what I believe and what I will refer to often. Nevertheless, this book is meant for leaders in every facet of life and any faith tradition or no faith tradition. Whatever name you give to the Source of Energy and Life within, that Source works with us to create a new world.

My emphasis on the good may lead people to believe that I am a Pollyanna, that I live in a fantasyland where all is bright and shiny and no dark invades my space. Nothing could be farther from the truth. Actually, at a personal level, I am more of a "glass is half empty" kind of person. I tend to see the negative before I become aware of the positive. And I am well aware of the horrible realities that exist in our world. But emphasizing the positive has become a grace-filled choice for me, one I have worked hard to make and continue to make every day. The good is all around us if we choose to find it and celebrate it. And why wouldn't we?

Grace shows up in each of our lives every moment of every day, whether it be simply in the air we breathe or in a deep encounter which transforms us. These sometimes ordinary, sometimes out-of-the-ordinary events are God's way of touching us. But these revelations are meant not only for each of us individually, but also for the larger world as well. It is thus the responsibility of each of us to share what we have been given.

This is where leadership comes in. What you won't find in this book are what I call management skills – things like efficiency, time management, fundraising, delegation, finances, etc. All of these things are important in their own way, but they don't define a leader, especially the type of leader we need today. Leadership is much more an art than a science. It involves using who I am to influence others to make the world a better place. In this book, I use many examples of ordinary people stepping forward to share and influence by what they have learned from their life experience and grace.

Recently Dan, one of our congregational partners in mission, asked about the progress of my book. I told him a little bit about it. Then I asked him, "Dan, when have you cheered for the good lately?" Dan drawled, "All the time, sister, all the time." This response really touched my heart. I realized that, though I'm trying to articulate in this book what cheering for the good looks like, people all around me have already been *cheer leaders* for the good.

So, in each chapter, I highlight what ordinary people answered when I asked them, "How or when did you cheer for the good lately?" Hopefully these quotes may inspire you as they did me. I also include reflection questions at the end of each chapter to invite you to ponder your call and help you shine a light on your role as a *cheer leader* for others. And if you are unfamiliar with some religious words I use, check out the glossary at the back of the book.

This book is my attempt to be a *cheer leader* for you. As I reflect on my own experiences and those of others, I want to provide inspiration for you to reclaim your power. I am cheering for all of you to become the best leaders you can be. Together we can discover the gifts, passions, and skills needed to change the world. Together we can notice the sparks of God continually creating new opportunities for growth. Are you ready?

"Every great dream begins with a dreamer.
 Always remember, you have within you the strength,
  the patience, and the passion to reach for the stars
   to change the world." (Harriet Tubman)

1
LEADING AS EVERYONE'S CALL

Yes, everyone is a leader. Although most of us don't consider ourselves leaders, we all are. The question is whether we lead consciously or unconsciously. Those who are in official leadership positions usually try to lead consciously. They set out to influence people. The rest of us who don't have official positions are also leaders, but often fail to acknowledge that we influence anyone. Consequently, we don't claim the title of leader. Kevin Kruse, in his book *Great Leaders Have No Rules*, encourages us to rethink this stance:

> "Leadership, with its endless definitions, is most often boiled down to one word: *influence*.... [You] influence people all the time, even without trying.... You influence others when you act, and when you stand by. You influence others when you speak up, and when you remain silent....
>
> [I]f leadership is influence, then leadership isn't a choice... The question is, are you influencing [people]

– leading them – in a positive direction or a negative direction. Be mindful of your power as a leader. Lead with intent." (Kruse, pp. 184, 194)

This is the first principle of good leadership – to influence others with positive intent wherever you are.

In all aspects of our lives, we play many roles. Sometimes we are followers and sometimes we assume the leadership role. But we always have the potential of leadership within us, the ability to influence people. This potential is played out through various leadership styles. Certain leadership styles are more appropriate for some situations rather than others. For example, in an emergency, EMTs will take charge, shout out commands, and expect to be obeyed. But in the ambulance on the way to the hospital, they may gently urge the victim to hang in there, to breathe, to marshal their own strength and resources. Kindergarten teachers also need to be in charge, but they would scare their students if they yelled at them in the classroom. However, if one of the students was running out into the street, the kindergarten teacher would definitely need to yell and demand "Stop!"

Each of these leaders, if they are good leaders, care about their followers and want them to embrace their own gifts and talents. They promote the potential in people, and help others to live into their particular call in life. Note these examples of people I know who are leaders in their own arenas, even if they often don't see themselves that way:

- Ann said, "I am not a leader." Really?! This is someone who is an active parent and grandparent, a former kindergarten teacher who cultivated potential in little minds for years, someone who reaches out on-line to

- people who advocate for causes she believes in, who brings food to needy people. In each and every one of these ways, Ann is a leader.
- Sister Claudia said, "I am not a leader." Really?! Here is someone who spent her whole professional life teaching primary school children. Here is someone who agreed to mentor a young adult who didn't think she had much to give. Here is someone who quietly goes about seeing good in people. Sister Claudia is a leader.
- David said, "In my job, my goal was not to be a leader. My goal was to accomplish our mission, and empowering the staff to use their talents was the best way to do it." He went beyond the job to welcome immigrant workers and cultivate a caring atmosphere in the workplace. David is a leader.
- Susan is the mother of a child with autism. She lives most of her days caring for and teaching her non-verbal child. In addition, she spends hours on-line and on the phone, researching programs, services, grants, and insurances that will support her child. Susan is a leader.
- Nick is a popular high school student. He is not on student council or in any other school group or club. But when his friends started to bully a new student, Nick said, "No!" Nick is a leader.

Each of these folks is intentionally influencing people in a positive direction. And they consider themselves one of the group, no better than their followers.

In the past, in institutions everywhere in the world – in families, churches, business, government, military – the leader was considered "better than" or "over" the people.

In a mechanistic age, it was the leader who commanded the workers to produce the most output with the greatest efficiency. The workers did not need to give input or share in groups. They just needed to be good followers. And it usually worked, especially if the leader cared about the followers and encouraged them to do their best. But in the process, people learned to focus too much on the executive. They looked to him to solve their problems, and they downplayed their own role in leadership.

Ivone Gebara, a Brazilian feminist philosopher and theologian, was asked back in 2001 what the most important spiritual question of the 21st century was. Her answer was this – the lack of confidence of the human person in the human person. She went on to state: "The spirit of submission and dependence is a sick spirit, a state contrary to the call of liberty contained in the depth of all human beings." (Snyder, p. 116) A good example of this is the U.S. elections, where in a country that proclaims "government of the people, by the people, and for the people," often only half of the eligible voters actually vote. People have ceded their rightful authority. As General Stanley McChrystal said, "Americans look to the wrong place for leaders; they need to look in the mirror." (Zakaria, Interview on CNN)

> "I was so nervous when I was asked to lead a group discussion, but I let everyone know that we would do this together." (Alice)

"Times have changed," as the saying goes. And with it, leadership needs to change. The old paradigm is not healthy for the group nor for the leader. Now the effective leader is not the one on the pedestal commanding the followers with the goal of producing a lot of the right product in the fastest way possible with no consideration of the cogs in the wheel.

No, the effective leader now inspires and encourages the followers to be their best selves and make use of their own gifts to achieve the mission. Such active engagement and close proximity between leader and followers create a common mission that everyone can buy into.

It is rewarding to recognize that a number of new leaders are already doing things differently. One is Jacinda Ardern, the Prime Minister of New Zealand. This millennial wasn't someone who planned to be out in front to the extent she is. Suddenly, in an unexpected twist of fate, she became the Prime Minister. In her first years of office, she was confronted with a mass shooting in a mosque, a newly-active volcano, and the coronavirus. Oh, and by the way, she also gave birth to her first child. In the midst of it all, she managed to convey to her citizens that she had their back. She did this by listening deeply and responding compassionately. Through kindness and inclusion, she managed to inspire others to work together and to be their best selves. Ardern is a *cheer leader* for her people. As Time magazine stated,

> "In other countries, voters have been drawn to strongmen and salesmen, wooed by the promise of simple answers to complex questions. People have lost trust in their institutions, whether they be government, media, organized religion or the scientific community. When voters feel powerless and disenfranchised, Ardern told Time…, 'we can either stoke it with fear and blame, or we can respond to it by taking some responsibility and giving some hope that our democratic institutions, our politicians actually can do something about what they're feeling.'" (Luscombe, *Time*, March 2-9, 2020)

This new leadership model has different underlying assumptions. For example, the leader doesn't have to know everything. In fact, acknowledging this fact goes a long way toward becoming an effective leader. That leader will come to know how important it is to depend on others. He or she must exercise deep listening and asking skills because there are always others who have suggestions or pledges of help and who just want to be asked. Leadership must focus on what's right with the world, not what's wrong with it. And most important of all, the leader must believe that everyone else is also a leader with much to give.

I like to use the term "a leader in every chair." This phrase comes from the book *The Circle Way: A Leader in Every Chair* by Christina Baldwin and Ann Linnea. Christina and Ann began a movement called The Circle Way in 1992, and it has spread around the world. It is based on the wisdom of native peoples, who met in a circle around the fire to discuss and decide important issues with everyone contributing. As quoted on the website *The Circle Way*, "We have always known that the circle is a natural way to gather for conversations. Circle is a democratic space where we can look each other in the eye, lean in and listen, and include all voices with a sense of equality." Everyone contributes his or her wisdom and listens to others contribute their wisdom in turn. Each has a piece of the truth. In this way, as Baldwin and Linnea state, "The practice of circle often leads to more creative options, wiser decisions, clearer actions."

Effective *cheer leaders* today influence the world in many different positive ways. Collectively, *cheer leaders* have the ability to rally people around a goal or mission. They don't say, "This is what I can do for you." Rather, they ask, "What can we do together?" And "how can we do it?" The last question is particularly important because not everyone has the experience or the knowledge of methods for organizing and facilitating. Many people have never been asked to share their wisdom in a group. So, in order to get the most response, the *cheer leader* may also need to become a mentor or a facilitator.

Just as cheerleaders are sometimes cheering out in the middle of the gym floor and sometimes on the sidelines, so too *cheer leaders* sometimes lead from the front and sometimes from behind the scenes. As a leader there were many times when I had to speak out publicly about an issue or respond to reporters' questions about an FSPA initiative. I had to articulate our FSPA mission so that people could understand and support it. I had to design processes which helped people get on board with our movement.

But even when I was out front as the designated leader, it wasn't all about me and my opinions and desires. It was always a group process, a melding and transforming of many ideas. I had to trust the process, that a greater wisdom had emerged through prayer, honest discussion, and contemplative decision making. Sometimes this was hard for me, because we all think our ideas are the best. Right? And we want to put them into practice, like right now. But, with our leadership team or in committee work, I needed to state my opinion and lobby for my vision, sometimes over and over, but then I needed to let it go to be shaped, fired, and purified by the group. It doesn't mean that I let go of my vision, but I accepted the group wisdom in that moment. I still was in front, carrying the message to the world. And many times, the result turned out to be much better than I could ever have imagined. At other times, the time was not ripe for my vision; it was too early. And surprisingly, sometimes the same basic idea or vision appeared years later, often through someone else, when we were all on the same page. Trusting in God's wisdom and God's own time helped greatly during these periods of waiting.

At other times, leaders step back and assume a more "behind the scenes" approach to *cheer leading*. An excellent example of this happened at our 2013 FSPA general assembly. Instead of the leadership team taking the lead in determining future ministries of the congregation, the facilitator used an "open space" approach. Anyone could initiate a discussion around a ministry idea in order to see if other people were interested. Amazingly, in two sessions, we had about 30 discussion groups, resulting in wonderful new ideas for ministry. We called them "action groups," and though all of the ideas did not come to fruition, some of our most vibrant collaborative ministry ventures at the present time came out of these sessions. This was truly an example of people assuming leadership and starting a movement. And what I did in my elected leadership role was to cheer them on. I cheered for them not only verbally and in writing, but by helping them get access to resources, communication vehicles, and a platform.

Back in high school, when we cheerleaders would be resting or taking it too easy, often some student would rise from the crowd and start a cheer. It was quite a comeuppance for us, but it was a sign of a healthy group – leadership waiting to spring up. We have seen a lot of *cheer leaders* springing up in our world today. Many times it's been our young people who have stepped forward. One key example is the Parkland, Florida high school students who organized a nationwide movement to ban assault weapons after the massacre at their school. Other recent movements begun by ordinary people have been "Black Lives Matter," the "Me Too" movement, and the service centers established at borders all over the world to aid migrants fleeing violence, drought, and persecution. As you see, everyone can be a leader.

Leadership today remains what it has always been, but it has new aspects. As Seth Godin says, "The power of this new era is simple: if you want to (need to, must!) lead, then you can. It's easier than ever and we need you." (Godin, p. 6) Technology has made it easier for anyone who wants to proclaim a view or start a movement to reach the public. But technology has also created challenges – cyber bullying, uncensored hate speech, false statements, an urgency that works against thinking things through. Even though the potentiality for influencing people for the good is quite available on social media platforms, too often we find ourselves going along with the most brash statements and the latest trending opinions. To reclaim our leadership, we need to slow down, research, and think things through carefully. We must learn to respond out of our deep values rather than react out of emotion. It takes a wise leader to negotiate these minefields. And that person can be you.

What would it be like if everyone claimed their power as a leader, if the only question people asked is, "In what areas of life do I have expertise or wisdom or common sense that I can share?" Or "Who or what group needs to be encouraged or taught what I know?" Often people need to be drawn out. They don't like to assert themselves. Or they honestly think that they have nothing valuable to share with the broader world. At times like these, it may be helpful to ask people to tell a story about a time when they actually did cheer for another person or conveyed to others some piece

> *"I volunteered to distribute food to those who had lost their jobs during the COVID-19 crisis."*
> *(Jose)*

of wisdom they had learned. Often through this process, they realize that they have indeed exercised leadership, and they feel good about it. I'm sure there will be many stories of ordinary people exercising their leadership during the COVID 19 crisis that can inspire us all.

Leadership is a limitless quantity and can be found everywhere, if people make that choice. Margaret Wheatley, a speaker and writer on leadership and organizational change, challenges us all:

> "Wherever you're working is where you can take a stand. You don't have to go looking for new places, other issues, compelling causes. If you're in a school, a financial firm, the UN, a refugee camp, a small non-profit, a church, a hospital – wherever you are, stay there and notice the abundance of warrior opportunities…, speaking up against unjust actions, influencing policies to address root causes, calling attention to new populations that need services… If we don't speak up, who will?" (Wheatley, pp. 262-263)

Give me an L – (L), give me an E – (E), give me an A – (A),

Give me a D – E – R – (D-E-R).

What does that spell?
LEADER – say it again,

LEADER – what are you?

A LEADER, A LEADER, A LEADER!!!

REFLECTION QUESTIONS

- Do you think of yourself as a leader? If not, why not?

- In what area(s) of your life do you influence people for the good?

- As a leader, what challenges have you encountered? How have you dealt with them? Have you been able to find the potential within the challenge?

2
FOCUSING THE ENERGY OF THE SPIRIT

Cheerleading in a small rural Catholic school in Iowa in the late 1960s was quite different from the practice and art of cheerleading today. No cartwheels, flips, pyramids, or elaborate dance routines for us. We weren't there to entertain; we were there to lead. In a simple way, we brought together a group of people for a common cause and inspired them to pursue their communal goal with energy and enthusiasm.

This description of the task of a cheerleader may be very different from the cheerleader stereotypes which are common today. I know, because when I tell people that I am writing a book on leadership based on cheerleading, they either laugh or scoff. Some even express resentment and hurt that they weren't considered good enough to be a cheerleader in high school. But in our complex and challenging world, we can no longer afford to indulge these stereotypes. We need leaders who cheer for the good and encourage others to share their own goodness. That's basically what cheerleaders do. And this is what effective leaders do today. These leaders are *cheer leaders*.

Energy is what it's all about, then and now. Energy can be negative or positive. We've all experienced the negative energy darting around during chaotic times: anger, fear, confusion, anxiety, leading to blaming and hate. With all that negative energy seeping into our psyches, people feel a dissipation of soul. They lose hope and feel sadness and helplessness. Thankfully, there is also much good energy surrounding us: love, joy, peace, patience, kindness, goodness, faithfulness, gentleness, and self-control. These are the attributes of a person or community living in accord with the Holy Spirit.

The Acts of the Apostles in the Christian Scripture describes Pentecost, the time when the followers of Jesus were gifted with the Spirit in a special way:

> "When the day of Pentecost had come, they were all together in one place. And suddenly from heaven there came a sound like the rush of a violent wind, and it filled the entire house where they were sitting. Divided tongues, as of fire, appeared among them, and a tongue rested on each of them. All of them were filled with the Holy Spirit and began to speak in other languages, as the Spirit gave them the ability." (Acts 2:1-4 NRSV)

Images from modern science describe the same powerful energy of the Spirit in today's language. Miriam Therese Winter, MMS, in her book *Paradoxology: Spirituality in a Quantum Universe*, expresses more beautifully than I ever could the effect of the Spirit on each of us: "Energy: seething, swirling, caroming chaotically and creatively… Hovering over and hurling forth, churning within and burning throughout. The Spirit of the living God in the form of energy." Winter goes on to say: "That originating blast of energy in the flaring forth of the cosmos is with us everywhere as the air we breathe, the fire within, the life force of our being and our serendipitous becoming." (Winter, pp. 69- 70) This is the energy that *cheer leaders* must tap into, to encourage all of creation to send forth the breath of the Spirit to bring life and hope to the world.

> *"Every day I pray for our government leaders asking God to give them wisdom and compassion." (Mary)*

Cheer leaders embody the life energy of their group. They feel what their followers feel; they are one with them. I encountered this dynamic when I was a cheerleader. It was exciting, but the challenge was not to get sucked in by all the heightened feelings or to cling to one agenda. As a cheerleading squad we learned to temper this urge through training and practice. We learned to focus on the mission. We chose to funnel the crowd's energy through ourselves into communal creative action. There were many times when we wanted to yell at the refs or tell the opposing coach to "shut up." But we didn't. We instead entreated the fans to join us in cheering for the team:

"Two bits, four bits, six bits, a dollar;

All for the New Hawks, stand up and holler!!"

I formally learned this process when I was a mental health therapist. I learned to feel the client's feelings in my body and psyche, but not get trapped in them. I used them as information about my client. In the same way, *cheer leaders* learn about their followers' hopes, dreams, and desires through feeling with them, and then use that information to focus the group's energy to accomplish their mission. A *cheer leader*, to me, is

not an expert or one who has all the answers. A good *cheer leader* is **not** egotistic, a show-off, or a bully. He/she doesn't come in with a rigid agenda. Rather, a good *cheer leader* listens to the crowd, discerns its enthusiasms, and recognizes what it needs in order to accomplish its goal. Then he/she gets in front of the movement and brings them together energetically as one force for good.

But what about when the group's energy is low, when encouraging the good in the group is met with exhaustion or downright apathy? I've encountered this phenomenon many times both as a cheerleader and as a *cheer leader*, in gyms, classrooms, and committee meeting rooms. It is one of the hardest things to deal with. The temptation is to allow oneself to give in to the weariness and boredom. But that is not what we are called to do as leaders. Our job as *cheer leaders* is to evoke and stoke the group's energy to do something good. Sometimes in these situations the leader needs to stop and switch gears. He or she might have the group take a break. Or an icebreaker might help. Get everyone to stand up and participate in a fun activity, no matter how foolish it may seem. Or one can always jump into cheerleader mode and lead the group in a cheer:

"Lean to the left, lean to the right,

Stand up, sit down,

Fight, fight, fight!!

Inevitably, the energy rises in the room as we laugh and move. Then the *cheer leader* uses that energy to carry on with the task at hand.

Seth Godin's book, *Tribes: We Need You to Lead Us*, was

the catalyst which really ignited my enthusiasm for what a group can do when a leader cheers for the good. I found the book right before I took on the leadership of my congregation. FSPA as a group was decreasing in numbers, and the congregation was discerning what that reality meant for us and for our mission in the world. I knew that telling the diminishment narrative and making decisions from that perspective would do nothing to get our sisters excited about the future. So, our leadership team began to *cheer lead*. We told a positive and inspiring story about who FSPA is and has been, our vibrancy in the past, and our potentialities for the future. We made sure everyone was involved in the discussions about the way forward and indicated the need for everyone's input. Then we proclaimed a new scenario where sisters could get on board (figuratively, of course) the spaceship to "Planet Future." We proposed actions which would honor our past but let go of things that were hindering us from meeting the needs of the world today. We cheered for new forms of ministry. Because of this process, you could feel the energy rise in the room as sisters renewed their hope in the future.

When referring to the energy for something, I have taken to using the word "enthusiasm" instead of "passion." Passion has become the "word du jour," but "enthusiasm," meaning "in God within," fits better with the Spirit's energy. I saw this word used in a different way when I read Barry Prizant's book, *Uniquely Human*. Prizant tells the story of a talk given by the mother of a child with autism. At the end of the talk, someone asked this question, "I'm curious about your daughter's obsessions. How have you dealt with them?" The mother replied, "Hmmm. We've always thought of them as *enthusiasms*." Another parent "saw enthusiasm as a source of potential rather than an impediment or a problem." (Prizant, p. 56)

Enthusiasm seeks the good, the innate potential. Positivity is what creates real excitement within a movement. Even when things don't go so well, the leader remains faithful to the common goal and even goes further. As Henry Kissinger stated, "The task of a leader is to get their people from where they are to where they have not been." The leader holds on to hope and constantly puts that message before the people and draws them forward.

Finding the good in other people raises the energy and the will to create even more good. My friend, Sister Charlotte, was someone who always cheered for others. It was her mission to uncover their talents and leadership potential. She always said, "If I don't work myself out of a job by the time I leave, I will have failed." From the moment she entered a ministry, she encouraged the development of potential and mentored people around her to embrace the mission and become leaders. She did that as a principal of a school in El Salvador, where the woman she trained is still in the ministry after 30 years. She did it in Moline, Illinois, where she worked herself out of a job in a parish because her co-workers assumed the leadership when she became ill. Charlotte taught me a valuable lesson: much of being a leader is evoking the leadership potential in others. As John Buchan, a novelist and public servant, said, "The task of leadership is not to put greatness into people, but to elicit it, for the greatness is there already."

> *"I love complimenting people on a wonderful service they have performed."* (Angela)

How do we elicit the greatness already there? Most basic of all is simple respect. Do we say "hi" when we meet people, and use their name when we can? Another great way to elicit greatness is to take time with people. So often as a leader I felt

I was too busy and walked right past people. But as often as I became aware of what I was doing, I made a choice to stop and engage. In this way, leaders come to know their followers and their stories and develop a relationship. Then when leadership opportunities arise, they know their strengths and gifts, and can call them forth to service. For example, in meetings, the leader could ask everyone to tell a story about someone who had inspired them, a risk they had taken, or a Spirit-led opportunity that had presented itself to them recently. In these ways, people are encouraged to claim their own gifts and strengths and be inspired by those of others.

Enthusiasm **for** something requires vision and caring deeply about certain things, but one doesn't need super knowledge or a rigid agenda to accomplish these goals. I remember when I became the lead person in welcoming new members to our congregation (what we call Director of Incorporation.) I had energy for the work, but I didn't necessarily know how to do it. Meanwhile, I was connecting with the new women, listening deeply to hear their longings, and facilitating their call to this new life. I realized, then, that I was already being a leader.

Furthermore, *cheer leading* involves being on a team. We don't do it alone. What one doesn't think of, the others will. When courage is required, we can stand together. Every leader should consider herself or himself part of a team. Being a lone wolf is dangerous for a leader today because the world is too complex for one person to have all the answers. A team fosters collaboration with others, where everyone brings their best ideas, listens with an open heart, and together something wonderful is created. I am forever grateful that I had a wonderful team to work with, both in my cheerleading in high school and in my congregational leadership.

Inspired *cheer leaders* look for and cheer for goodness everywhere. As Richard Rohr, OFM, wrote: "All of the world is sacred…. Our job as humans is to make admiration of others and adoration of God fully conscious and deliberate. It is the very purpose of life." (Rohr, *Eager to Love*, p. 10) Christian Scriptures challenge us to the same thing:

> "The Spirit of God is upon me. I have been anointed to bring good news to the poor, to proclaim release to the captives, and recovery of sight to the blind, to liberate those who are oppressed, to proclaim the year of favor." (Luke 4:18-19 NAB)

The mission of a *cheer leader*, should you choose to accept it, is to go forth to lead others with enthusiasm and the energy of the Spirit.

REFLECTION QUESTIONS

- What do you do when you sense negative energy around you?

- Remember a time when the leader(s) of a group you were in cheered you on and gave you hope for the future. How did you feel and act?

- When have you fostered the leadership potential in another?

3

RECLAIMING GOODNESS

I loved high school cheerleading! It was always so much fun to go to the games and be so intimately involved in the action. And it was so positive! We were stoking positive energy, not bringing people down, even when the game wasn't going particularly well. It was our job to be upbeat, look for the good, and foster hope. It felt great!

But remember what I said about being somewhat of a "glass is half empty" type person? It wasn't always so easy for me to be positive. I could easily slip into the negative. Here's a perfect illustration: in 2005 I won prizes on the TV game show "The Price is Right." It was so much fun and I was so excited! But immediately afterward, my joy quickly morphed into anxiety – how was I going to pay the luxury taxes on the prizes? What would I tell my community? Really?!! My friend Joann was flabbergasted that I could flip so fast to the negative. She became my *cheer leader*. She said, "Focus on the positive! Just enjoy it."

Fast forward to June, 2018. With our world in a state of

chaos and suffering, our sisters and affiliates decided on this title for our quadrennial mission gathering: "A REVOLUTION OF GOODNESS!!" With these words, three hundred FSPA sisters, affiliates, employees, other partners in mission, and invited guests from all over the country committed to spending the weekend of June 1-3 focusing on goodness and pledging ourselves to look for it everywhere.

We told stories and asked challenging questions. "Recall and tell the story of a time when you were part of something that recognized the goodness of all." "What comes to mind when you imagine a person of goodness?" "What are the needs of today?" "How can an emphasis on goodness change the world?" We came away with group commitments to such actions as these: "I proclaim 'A Revolution of Goodness' by...

- being present to and with the marginalized;
- building small group faith communities;
- giving others the space to speak rather than deciding what they need from our place of privilege;
- standing shoulder to shoulder with Muslims, Jews, and all faith traditions;
- practicing kindness to the earth;
- empowering others to identify their Unique Goodness to be shared with the world."

We became *cheer leaders* for the good. We proclaimed a revolution of goodness!

What is goodness? The dictionary states that goodness is "the state of being morally good or virtuous." While this is true, I expand the definition of goodness by taking it back to the very beginning of creation. There God created everything and declared, "It is good." To me this suggests that everything in creation is basically good. When we sin, we lose our way from our true path and hurt ourselves and others, but underneath, our basic goodness remains.

So why would our gathering in 2018 have been considered such a revolution? First of all, Richard Rohr, OFM, has pointed out in his book, it often feels natural for us to go straight for the negative. I guess it's a cave-person self-preservation instinct alive and well today. It served a purpose in ancient times to avoid danger; it helped us survive. But that's not typically the case now. As Rohr states, citing the work of neuroscientist Rick Hanson:

> "Brain studies have shown that we may be hardwired to focus on problems at the expense of a positive vision. The human brain wraps around fear and problems like Velcro. We dwell on bad experiences long after the fact, and spend vast amounts of energy anticipating what might go wrong in the future. Conversely, positivity and gratitude and simple happiness slide away like cheese on hot Teflon." (Rohr, *The Universal Christ*, pp. 63-64)

To make it worse, the prevailing Christian religious practice has emphasized sin and evil. As a kid in church, I never heard that I was good; I heard over and over again that I was a sinner. Influenced by the theory of original sin, by theologians and reformers who expanded on this, and by Freudian-based psychology which emphasized a person's pathology rather than strengths, I would bet that most people in the Christian West can't bear to believe in their basic goodness. It feels too prideful and vulnerable. Women especially have trouble with this since throughout history women have been seen as basically flawed, lesser than men, and told to stay in the background. Too often they've learned their lesson too well.

The result has been that toxic shame has become the norm in our society. Toxic shame is the inner sense of feeling flawed or insufficient as a person, the very antithesis of believing in one's goodness. Having been told by religion, society, and family that one is not good enough, the experience of shame goes very deep. One experiencing toxic shame will try to hide and protect themselves, or on the other hand, will lash out in anger and blame at the world. Either way, the person loses connection with themselves and with others. Brené Brown, who has researched and written much on vulnerability and shame, described our situation this way:

> "[Shame] is becoming an increasingly divisive and destructive part of our culture... Name calling and character assassinations have replaced national discussions about religion, politics and culture ... [E]xclusion and public humiliation consistently grab the top ratings.... The culture of shame is driven by fear, blame and disconnection...." (Brown, *I Thought It Was Just Me (But It Isn't)*, p. xix)

That's why our gathering chose to proclaim an alternate reality, an "upside-downness," as Richard Rohr calls it. While much of the world is focused on the bad, our movement states that we are good, and goodness can be found everywhere. "Once we can accept that

> *"I stood up to the school when they treated my 6-year-old son as a behavior problem rather than as a good kid with a learning disability."* (Lindsay)

God is in all situations, and can and will use even bad situations for good, then everything becomes an occasion for good and an occasion for God...." (Rohr, *Eager to Love,* p.10) We just have to choose it.

Our congregation decided to follow up on the summer gathering by continuing the focus on goodness throughout our entire FSPA culture. We chose Appreciative Inquiry as a method to accomplish the goal and hired a facilitator to lead us. Appreciative Inquiry, introduced by David Cooperrider and his associates at Case Western Reserve University, is the study and exploration of what gives life to human systems when they function at their best. It differs from the traditional approach to organizational change which focuses on what's wrong or broken. The Appreciative Inquiry approach, in contrast, focuses on what's right in the organization or with the person and builds on it. It asks positive questions like these:

- What is really working well in your life (job) right now? How can you build on it?
- Who has inspired you recently? What was the goodness you witnessed?
- Tell me about a time when you practiced good leadership. What did you learn from this experience?

We began to use questions like these in staff gatherings, performance evaluations, meetings, newsletters, and many other venues. After performance evaluations, I actually saw staff members stand taller. The result of our efforts has been an increased unity where people feel good about themselves, and therefore feel called to step forward and share their talent or insight. More people are claiming their own leadership.

One premise of Appreciative Inquiry that has particularly

stood out for me is this one: "What you focus on becomes your reality." If I focus on the negative, my reality will consist of anger, frustration, despair, powerlessness, and a lack of creative energy. But if I focus on the positive, I will be energized, upbeat, hopeful, creative, and I will naturally attract other energetic people. *National Geographic* photographer DeWitt Jones embodies this approach. He has created a number of beautiful videos and books, sending the message to "Celebrate What's Right with the World." After repeatedly viewing these videos, I always come away inspired and invigorated to find the good all around me. Two quotes from DeWitt stay with me:

- "I learned to reframe obstacles into opportunities by putting a lens of celebration on my camera."
- "Every day we can choose the lens we want to use: do we want to ask, "What's the matter with our world?" or do we ask, "What's right in this situation?"

If we focus on the goodness in every situation, we will tap into the energy of the Spirit, and that energy is powerful. Personally, I have spent years deconstructing my instinctive negative view of life. Through grace and hard work, I have been able to say "no" to a belief that I am not enough, that others are somehow a threat to me, or that God is a harsh judge. I have said "yes" to my own goodness, to a natural curiosity and attraction to others, and to a trust in God as Loving Presence always with me.

As I have opened myself more to looking for the good, good has come to me. I recently met a non-verbal 8-year-old girl with autism. My heart was drawn to her, and I wanted to understand her and connect. That opening to goodness led me to read some books written by parents of children with autism (and sometimes even the person themselves). Then I found a book by Dr. Barry M. Prizant called *Uniquely Human: A Different Way of Seeing Autism* (which I mentioned earlier.) This book attributes to people with autism what I've believed about all people – that we aren't random or deviant or bad; we are all gifted with a wonderful life energy. We just need people in our corner to listen deeply to us, to cheer for us, and to offer support in finding our meaning and purpose. This unexpected book has inspired me to continue opening myself to the goodness present everywhere, even in the least expected places.

This focus on the good has been gathering momentum for many years. I think it's because we as a people are being overwhelmed by the negative, and we realize that we need an alternative if we are to survive. For example, there's a show on public radio which asks listeners to leave a message about the best thing that happened to them that week. There are the network news segments, like "Inspiring America" on NBC Nightly News, which end the news broadcast on a much-needed high note. Positive psychology, begun in 1998 by Martin Seligman, puts an emphasis not on mental illness or disorders, but on happiness, well-being, and flourishing. It focuses on the "good life," in which you use your strengths "to produce authentic happiness and abundant gratification."

In the area of social change, the concept of "positive deviance" is based on the work of Jerry Sternin with childhood nutrition in Vietnam in the 1990s. Instead of focusing on the malnourished children, in other words, on the problem, as other workers did, he focused on positive behaviors. Sternin asked, "Why are some children in the same situation healthy?" And he didn't ask experts. He asked mothers in the village if any of them had well-nourished children, and when a few raised their hands, he asked them what they did differently. Then, he and his team used this knowledge to teach the other mothers, which led to significant behavior changes in the villages. Sternin directed his attention to the positive, what was already working in the groups, in order to bring about life-changing results.

This focus on the good in various disciplines signals the way forward for all of us. Each of us must make daily choices to focus on the good. Along with our personal choices, we need leaders with creative ideas and methods of leadership which tap into the best of our human instincts rather than the worst.

> *"When a discussion deteriorated into a blaming game, I re-directed the conversation."* (Bud)

You, too, can choose to focus on what's right with the world, rather than what's wrong with it. You, too, can choose to see every "problem" as an opportunity. You, too, can choose to open yourself to goodness everywhere. Whether you laud the good deeds of your employees, point out a strength in your children, or bring positive energy to a community planning session, you can be a *cheer leader* for positive change. The world is waiting for you to act. As James Hoggan wrote:

> "People are not inspired by prophecies of doom, so we need to start painting pictures of a better future, telling positive narratives that expand what people see as possible, that engage people and give them a feasible alternative to the status quo." (Hoggan, "Speak the Truth, but Not to Punish")

"We are good, yes we are;

We are good and so are you.

We are good, yes we are;

We are good and so are you.

No more jeering;

No more shame.

Find the good and we all win."

REFLECTION QUESTIONS

- Remember a person in your life who always seemed to focus on the good. What effect did he/she have on you?

- Think of a time when you were able to reframe an obstacle into an opportunity. How did that change your feelings and actions?

- Name three things that are "right with the world."

4
SEARCHING FOR MEANING AND PURPOSE

Why am I here? This is the most fundamental question any of us can ask ourselves. If we don't have some inkling of our purpose or the meaning of life, what's the point? Unfortunately, this is the exact place where too many find themselves today.

When chaos seems to rule, facts don't seem to matter, and everything is changing so fast that we often can't keep up, more than ever people are searching for meaning or purpose in their lives. When churches no longer convey relevancy, when institutions become so corrupt that trust is assaulted, when families are so far apart either physically or emotionally that they struggle to reinforce core family values, people often sink into despair, addiction, anger, apathy, or greed. These can all be results of desperate searches to find some meaning in life that they can hold on to.

Cheerleaders are most needed when all hope seems to be lost, when the team has a losing record, and the players and fans have become dispirited. This is the time when cheerleaders must go out and yell out the most focused and powerful cheer they have. This cheer for our cheerleading squad in high school was this:

"F-F-F-I-G, G-G-G-H-T!!

F-I-G, G-H-T, Fight Team Fight!!"

We'd stomp our feet and yell loudly to wake everyone up and point again to our mission. "Hey, the team needs us! Let's go!" I can still feel the gym floor quake and the bleachers rumble and the rafters echo the roaring sound back to us. No one could sleep through that!

Now, at this time in history, I shout again, "Hey, the team needs us! Let's go!" This is our purpose in life. This time the "team" is our planet and all its creatures, its institutions, its families. They need us to be *cheer leaders*, to call attention to the needs all around us, to proclaim "we can make things better; there is a future!" As Viktor Frankl stated: "There is nothing in the world ... that would so effectively help one to survive even the worst conditions as the knowledge that there is a meaning in one's life."

> *"I joined the League of Women Voters to cheer for democracy."* (Gail)

Meaning-making is a very human pursuit. We are always searching for purpose and meaning in our lives, our relationships, our institutions, our professions. As a matter of fact, I was listening to public radio the other day, and one of the guests on the show reported that the word "purpose" had replaced "happiness" as the top search item for a life value. This shows where people's hearts and longings lie.

At different points in our lives, we stop, look back, and

try to make sense of what has happened. We arrange these events into a coherent whole, something that makes sense to us. Then we tell stories, create art or music, write, dance, or arrange a scrapbook. These creations provide an anchor of new awareness as we move forward. For me, writing this book at this time is helping me to make meaning from my life and my many years of leadership.

For institutions, especially during polarized times like these, it is helpful to tap into group history, identity, and values. This exercise is not meant to rigidly cling to the past. It is, rather, a way to ground ourselves, to ask why we were founded, what are our common values, and how circumstances have changed since the beginning of our group which are calling for new responses. This looking back provides clarity for the now and a sense of purpose and stability needed to reach for the future.

A good example of this continual search for meaning from our FSPA history involves Mother Ludovica Keller. The year was 1926. Mother Ludovica was 82 years old and had already been the leader of FSPA for 44 years. During her tenure the congregation had expanded and stabilized. Sisters were involved in prayer, the care of orphans, teaching at all levels, nursing, and catechizing all over the country. I don't know about you, but at this point I would have wanted to sit back, put my feet up, and be satisfied with what had been accomplished. But then a diocesan representative from Wuhan, China showed up in Mother Ludovica's office requesting sisters to start a school and minister in his diocese. She could have said, "We'd like to help you, but we need to preserve the good work we are already doing. We can't afford to spare any sisters." But she didn't say that. After much prayer, consultation, and discernment, she said "yes." She recognized the request as a call from God, just like the many other calls the congregation had received through the years. This was our mission – to not grow complacent and self-satisfied, but to recognize the needs of the world and respond to them with our presence, resources, and service. In 1928, six sisters embarked on the long journey to Wuhan, China, further solidifying our purpose.

We FSPA as a congregation have continued to ask through the years "What are the signs of our times?" and "What are we called to do and be now?" This quest has at root been a search for meaning. What makes our life and mission worthwhile? How do we continue to be relevant in our service to God's people at this time in history?

In more recent years, an answer to these questions emerged for us in a grace-filled, spontaneous, and "chance" encounter between Sister Marla, the elected leader of FSPA, and Sister Anna, the elected leader of the Tertiary Sisters of St. Francis (TSSF) from Cameroon, West Africa. During an international Franciscan meeting in Assisi in 1997, Marla and Anna were seated at the same table, and connected at a deep level. At one point, Anna courageously asked, "What could we do together?"

The TSSF were coming into their own. They had been indoctrinated with Western notions of Catholicism and religious life. Now emerging from the colonial influence, what the TSSF desired was to discover how to claim their own meaning and purpose in their own particular culture and setting with its own particular needs. What they desired was a deepening process of claiming themselves as African Franciscan women religious. And they asked us to help.

It just so happened that FSPA and two other U.S. congregations who had split from each other years back were working toward reconciliation at that very time. As part of that process, the leaders had asked, "How can we together reach out to each other, but at the same time go beyond that?" The serendipitous meeting between Sisters Marla and Anna seemed like an answer. Following the Spirit, the four congregations officially formed the Franciscan Common Venture (FCV) in 1999. Through more than 20 years this collaborative relationship has given new life and meaning to all four congregations. We engaged in global sisterhood. It was through relationship with each other that we all came to a new appreciation of our call in this present moment.

It was a privileged encounter, but it wasn't always easy. The temptation for us Americans was often to impose our way of doing things unto them, because, as you know, we always think our way is best! One tiny example comes from my experience of visiting Cameroon in 2012. My task was to use my gifts and skills as a pastoral counselor to teach, facilitate, and cheer for a group of sisters participating in a renewal program. At first, I relied heavily on the written word in my teaching. I soon realized, however, that the Cameroonian sisters came from an oral culture. What made sense to them was not necessarily reading articles and writing notes, but storytelling, singing and dancing, and passing on wisdom from the past. Another example was my experience of religious life. While many of my examples from my own experience might have been helpful to them, I had to remember to constantly ask them to tell me about their own lived experience of religious life. That's where the seeds for growth lay for them. By listening and learning from one another, we became *cheer leaders* for each other and better *cheer leaders* for the world.

Another way God helped FSPA to deepen our own sense of purpose and meaning was inviting us to claim our common mission with the lay people. One example where this played out was in our decision in 2017, after many years of questioning and discerning, to hand over the sponsorship of our hospitals and university to the lay leaders of these institutions. Sponsorship in religious institutions is the relationship whereby the religious congregation continues to influence the publicly incorporated institutions that they founded. By handing over sponsorship, we FSPA were proclaiming that we trusted the lay leadership of each institution to carry on the Franciscan mission that we had handed on to them. This allowed us to focus our energies more in the area of working with the marginalized and poor, the Earth, and our global brothers and sisters.

> *"I wrote my senator asking her to support the DACA legislation. This is the only home the Dreamers have ever known."*
> (Patrick)

This was a major decision. People had for many decades associated women religious with the administration of schools and hospitals. Sisters were indeed needed in the 19th and 20th centuries to serve the European immigrants and give them the tools to integrate into our U.S. culture and society. Now, that has been accomplished. Yes, there is still a need to provide healthcare and education to people. But our lay partners are equipped to do that. Now, the people who really need us are those marginalized in society today and in places where the Spirit is sparking new life. FSPA heard that call, claimed the meaning it has for us, and chose to respond by adjusting our focus.

There are many examples where ordinary people like you and I have searched for meaning and purpose in challenging situations and ended up inspiring others to seek the purpose of their own lives. Viktor Frankl's book *Man's Search for Meaning* has become the iconic exploration of finding meaning in life when all forces seem to be working against it. Frankl, an Austrian Jewish psychiatrist, spent three years in Nazi concentrations camps, where he and his fellow prisoners tried to cling to life, meaning, and hope in the midst of de-humanizing and soul-crushing experiences. What he discovered for himself and others was that there had to be a reason for people to continue on. Otherwise, they soon gave up hope and died, literally or figuratively. Frankl stated:

> "What we really needed was a fundamental change in our attitude toward life. We had to learn ... that *it did not really matter what we expected from life, but rather what life expected from us.* We needed to stop asking about the meaning of life, and instead to think of ourselves as those who were being questioned by life – daily and hourly. Our answer must consist, not in talk and meditation, but in right action and in right conduct. Life ultimately means taking responsibility to find the right answer to its problems and to fulfill the tasks which it constantly sets for each individual." (Frankl, pp. 76-77)

After his personal struggle to find meaning, Frankl decided to write his famous book, not because he wanted to be famous, but because he wanted to encourage others to discover the questions that life posed for them. Frankl went on to develop logotherapy, a psychotherapy based on finding meaning in life. He, in other words, became a *cheer leader* for many others.

Each of us individually is called to continue searching for where life is calling us. This means becoming conscious, really conscious, of the world around us and the gifts we have to offer it. And, above all, it means that we recognize that there is a Power greater than ourselves. In my own life, I depend on God for everything. The basis of my life is prayer. I begin every day with these words: "O God, open my lips, and my mouth will proclaim your praise." And I end my day with "thank you." Everything in between and through the night depends on God and not on me. This provides a huge comfort for me as a leader.

I'll leave you with the prayer of Ghost Wolf, a Lakota pipe carrier in the 19th century:

> "If my people have a prayer for you, it is that you would wake up tomorrow and walk this world consciously. I pray that every moment you make will have a purpose. That every word you speak have a meaning and that every thought you have be a prayer."

REFLECTION QUESTIONS

- Recall a time in your life when you struggled to find meaning and purpose. What was the outcome?

- How has embracing a purpose in life influenced your leadership journey?

- Think of an example when relying on God or your Higher Power has strengthened your own sense of purpose in your life.

5
BELIEVING IN OUR ONENESS

The power in cheerleading comes from a group of fans being united in one loud voice. A single voice is not going to be heard in the din of a game. And many disparate voices will just create noise and confusion. So the cheerleaders must believe in the energy of the people, tap into their desire to energize their team, and somehow unite them in one loud insistent voice.

This is also our mission as *cheer leaders* today. We must bring together the voices of the whole planet – the croak of the frogs, the roar of the lion, the hiss of the snake, the weeping of the rain forest, the rustling of the wind, the steadfast silence of the rocks, the cry of the poor, the laughter of children. Each voice is equally important. Recently I attended a talk where members of the audience were urged "to get to know our seven billion siblings." This statement challenged and intrigued me. If all the peoples of the world plus all the rest of creation are my brothers and sisters, what difference does that make to me? How does it affect my life and the life of the planet?

As a Franciscan, I have been steeped in St. Francis' love of all creation. According to Franciscan priest Richard Rohr, St. Francis of Assisi "was, as far as we know, the first Christian to call animals and elements and even the forces of nature by familial names: 'Mother Earth,' 'Brother Wind,' 'Sister Water,' and 'Brother Fire.'" (Rohr, *The Universal Christ*, p. 112) Even so-called enemies, like the Sultan, were treated like relatives. This familial sense and call to love all have been foundational for many of us who follow his way.

But as the suffering of the planet grows – the disappearance of many plant and animal species, the widening gap between rich and poor, the melting of the glaciers through global climate change – the truth of our oneness with all creation is becoming more demanding of action. We don't have the luxury of naively clinging to our St. Francis birdbaths anymore. We can no longer afford to think of ourselves as separate. We must act now! It requires a love for our planet that goes beyond self-centeredness and partisanship.

We've heard this call to act on behalf of our planet many times before. For example, back in 1988, Joseph Campbell, a proponent of learning from our myths, presaged our present situation. "The only myth that is going to be worth thinking about in the immediate future is one that is talking about the planet, not the city, not these people, but the planet, and everybody on it." (Campbell, with Bill Moyers, p.32) It's been over 30 years since those words were uttered, but how many of us have gotten on board with this global thinking? I'm afraid too few.

Now we have a Swedish teenager, Greta Thunberg, forcefully pleading with world leaders at the United Nations and around the globe to do something to save the planet **now**. She scolded, "We are in the beginning of a mass extinction. And all you can talk about is money and fairy tales of eternal economic expansion. How dare you!!" Many people, especially young people, have been energized to action by her words. But, at the same time, she often receives hate mail. A national columnist recently wondered why we should listen to a

> *"I wrote a letter to the editor about the urgent need for climate change legislation."* (Margaret)

child. It seems to be so difficult for some to embrace the responsibility of all of us to care for Mother Earth. But Greta feels this responsibility in her bones and acts on it. These are the words the editors of *Time* used to laud her efforts:

> "For sounding the alarm about humanity's predatory relationship with the only home we have, for bringing to a fragmented world a voice that transcends backgrounds and borders, for showing us all what it might look like when a new generation leads, we name Greta Thunberg *Time* magazine's 2019 Person of the Year."

Thank God Pope Francis has also emerged as a *cheer leader* for the planet. By taking the name Francis, he symbolically raised St. Francis' love of all of creation to highest importance. His encyclical, *Laudato Si*, is an inspiring foundational document for all of us as we act to save the planet. He states: "Everything is connected. Concern for the environment thus needs to be joined to a sincere love for our fellow human beings and an unwavering commitment to resolving the problems of society.'" (#91) He goes on to say that in order to embrace our connectedness, we as humans "must regain the conviction that we need one another, that we have a shared responsibility for others and the world...." (#229)

This leads us to the notion of "the common good," an old concept, but one that is increasingly difficult to embrace in our individualistic and consumerist society. The common good is defined as the benefit or interests of **all**. We need each other. I love this quote from Luciano de Crescenzo: "We are each of us angels with only one wing, and we can only fly by embracing one another."

But, too often, the common good has been seen through the lens of those in power, what's good for the rich, the "in" race, the powerful institutions. Leaders have taken it upon themselves to define what the people and the earth need without listening to their constituents' actual needs and desires. But the common good calls us to see the larger picture, the true reality. We are all one. What will benefit everyone? How can we work together to achieve it?

The common good implies an embrace of diversity. But welcoming diversity can get messy. And yet, welcoming our diversity often strengthens our unity. When I was a cheerleader there were times when the energy in the gym against the opposing team rose to such a dangerous level that our cheerleading squad felt the urgent call to do something. We immediately went out on the floor and tried to channel the emotions into something positive and productive, not **against** something, but **for** something.

"I say black and you say gold;

(cheerleaders) BLACK!

(fans) GOLD!

(cheerleaders) BLACK!

(fans) GOLD!

I say shoot and you say two;

(cheerleaders) SHOOT!

(fans) TWO!

(cheerleaders) SHOOT!

(fans) TWO!

This cheer usually succeeded in focusing the energy of the fans where it needed to be.

In these polarized times, I am not looking for leaders with specific plans or ideas (although sometimes that is necessary and helpful). What I am looking for are leaders who understand and appreciate their followers, who can listen to all sides, and somehow bring people together. We in the U.S. have learned in recent elections that whole swaths of the electorate don't feel heard. Candidates have great ideas, but if they aren't willing or able to listen to the needs and desires of all their constituents, they are missing the boat (and also the election.)

A great example of this bringing people together across the divide was facilitated by the Franciscan Spirituality Center (FSC) in La Crosse after the 2016 presidential election. FSC sponsored a free program called "Post-Election Listening Session." Here's what the ad for it said:

"Even though the election is over, people are still divided and upset. Friendships are threatened, families are fighting; some are celebrating, others are grieving.

Join us for a listening session to express your feelings, strive to understand others' viewpoints, and look for signs of hope, courage and healing – no matter what side of the political spectrum you are on." The FSC staff began the session with a silent centering and a prayer. Then each person had 3 minutes to speak in a small group about their feelings regarding the election, with no interruptions, followed by a short pause before the next speaker. Following this, in the large group each person was invited to share 1 or 2 words that signified the hope or the challenge moving forward. A prayer for peace closed the session. Many attendees reported leaving the room feeling lighter and more hopeful.

Many times a *cheer leader* needs to use their role as facilitator to help people who don't have experience expressing their thoughts and feelings in a group. It is often helpful to start a meeting with a check-in, where everyone is asked to briefly share how they are feeling at that moment as they enter the meeting. This helps people settle in and be able focus on the work ahead. For first-timers, asking for just a word or phrase breaks the ice. Also, during a meeting, a leader who knows his/her followers can say something like this: "Joan, I know that you reach out to people when you volunteer at the hospital. How might that experience reveal some wisdom for all of us?"

This is a time of great change in the world with a resulting consolidation of new identity. Who are we now? This question parallels what we asked ourselves as teenagers. Sometimes then, to make ourselves feel better, we would form a clique, an exclusive group of people where we felt protected and had an identity. The problem came when we excluded others who didn't fit in, or, even worse, when we would bully them so we felt more powerful. This feels to me exactly like what many nations of the world, including the U. S, are struggling with right now. Who are we in this new global environment? How do we deal with our anxiety and fear? If we have leaders who aren't strong enough or skilled enough to lead us through these chaotic times with maturity and calm, we see the rise of hate speech, exclusion, and restrictive laws trying to keep "the other" in check. Is this who we want to be?

All of us need to make the leap of consciousness from the Separate to the One. No longer is it useful or even moral to think of ourselves as working in our own separate little universes. It's not us vs. them, conservatives vs. liberals, leaders vs. followers. We are on this journey of co-creation and transformation together. We each have our own particular expression of service and mission, but we need each embodied expression in order to bring about God's reign.

The title of the rule (or constitutions) my congregation of sisters lives by is *Unity in Diversity*. I'm always amazed that we could have chosen such an apt title and creed to live by back in the 1970s and still have it remain incredibly inspiring today. Embracing our unity in diversity today involves making connections with those who are different from us, be that differences in race, class, nationality, gender identity, language, or species. Getting out of one's comfort zone is difficult but can be embraced as exciting and transforming. Our congregation and our affiliates are embracing our "Unity in Diversity" in new ways. For example, we have partnered with others in our city to stand shoulder to shoulder with our Muslim and Hispanic brothers and sisters. We have pledged ourselves to unveiling our white privilege, and consequently are reading and discussing books like *White Fragility* by

Robin DiAngelo and *Waking Up White* by Debby Irving. Sisters and affiliates are going to the U.S.-Mexican border to help the migrants and inform the rest of us of the reality of the situation there. We are listening to our land and working to protect the environment. In all these ways, we ourselves are being transformed. We are seeing the universe as bigger than ourselves. And we are searching for the common good.

> *"I suggested to our facilities manager the benefits of using environmentally friendly cleaning products."*
> (Roy)

Let's cheer for all of creation, for all our brothers and sisters. We could adapt the theme song of the Pittsburgh Pirates which inspired them to win the World Series in 1979. It was called "We Are Family" sung by Sister Sledge. Together now, let's cheer with this version, over and over until we believe:

"WE ARE FAMILY!! I GOT ALL MY SISTERS [AND BROTHERS] WITH ME!

WE ARE FAMILY!! GET UP EVERYBODY AND SING.

WE ARE FAMILY!! I GOT ALL MY SISTERS [AND BROTHERS] WITH ME!

WE ARE FAMILY!! GET UP EVERYBODY AND SING.

REFLECTION QUESTIONS

- Remember a time when you consciously connected with one of your planetary siblings whom you hadn't interacted with before. What did you learn?

- What did Pope Francis mean when he said that humans "must regain the conviction that we need one another, that we have shared responsibility for others and the world"?

- When as a leader have you been challenged by diversity? How did you handle it?

6
EMBRACING VULNERABILITY

Going out on the floor during a basketball game in front of lots of people is a vulnerable position. I wasn't the prettiest or the most popular or the fittest. I often lacked confidence. But I loved sports and I wanted to be involved in the action. (Unfortunately, our school didn't have girls' sports at that time.) I often found myself going home and imitating the cheerleaders. While I was drying dishes with my mom, I would tell her about the new routine I had thought up. I would even demonstrate it (but not before I put the dish down.) I felt the cheer surge through my body, and I felt powerful. At some point I decided I could be a real cheerleader. So, I practiced hard and tried out in my junior year. I was able to put aside my feelings of "not-enoughness" and bring my whole self to the task of cheerleading. Remarkably, I was chosen! What a happy day!

Fast forward to a few years ago. It was 6:00 p.m. and another social event found me wandering around the crowd, not making eye contact. I was the elected leader of my religious congregation, and as such was often invited to dinners and socials put on by our sponsored ministries and the local non-profits. I found these events excruciatingly difficult. My old vulnerability of not feeling good enough arose. I would have much rather given a speech than mingle with people, many of whom I didn't know. Who will I talk to? What will I say? How do I approach? But this time, with a little encouragement from others beforehand, I adopted an undefended demeanor, revealing an openness to engagement. I cheered myself on: "You can do this. You want to talk with some interesting people. You want to make connections." So, I stopped circling and approached a couple who were standing by themselves. I claimed my vulnerability as a way to forge connection. I said, "I come to these things a lot and barely know anyone. I thought I'd come up and say 'hi' and introduce myself." They were totally receptive. They said they often felt the same way. We went on to have a delightful conversation! And then I moved on and did it again.

This experience taught me a lot about leadership. A leader doesn't always come from a position of strength. He/she has both strengths and vulnerabilities. It's what the leader does with them that makes all the difference. It's a matter of choice. When the leader can accept both his/her strengths and vulnerabilities, that leader will bring his or her whole person to their mission. And that leader will assure the followers that it's okay to not be perfect, that they are valuable no matter what.

"Whether we win or whether we lose,

This is the cheer we always use:

N-E-W-H-A-W-K-S!

New Hawk! New Hawks! New Hawks!"

One woman who made the choice to share both her strengths and her vulnerabilities is Alice Holstein. Alice has a doctorate in education, served as a college instructor, an officer in the Air Force, and a peer support specialist. AND, Alice has a severe mental illness with which she has struggled most of her life, to the point of living on the streets at one time. But Alice discovered a path to healing, which included being welcomed, heard, and encouraged to share her gifts which allowed her to open up and accept herself. As Alice said, "One of the most important things I did to promote my healing was to reframe my experience." She began to see that her vulnerabilities were also her strengths. She began to de-stigmatize mental illness and become a vocal advocate for mental health awareness. She has written many essays and is the author of three books. One is *Tough Grace: Mental Illness as a Spiritual Path*. As she said in referring to the book, "If we believed that this was a journey of hardship and suffering that was noble and worthy of the highest esteem, then things could be radically different. This is a revolutionary viewpoint." (Speech given in receiving the "Shining Star Award from the Mental Health Coalition of Greater La Crosse.)

The Gospels show that Jesus himself also revealed both his strength and his vulnerabilities. His humanness drew people to him and led to their healing. One of our FSPA affiliates, Vince Hatt, wrote about this in the *La Crosse Tribune*:

> "I saw how often Jesus was vulnerable [in the Gospels]. He cried over Jerusalem. His insides were torn up at the death of Lazarus. He humbly washed the feet of his disciples. He risked death in his hometown. He agonized in the garden. He cried in a loud voice from the cross, 'My God, my God, why have you forsaken me?'

To follow Jesus means to be vulnerable." (Hatt, "The Power of Being Vulnerable)

The dictionary defines vulnerability as the state of being open to attack or the possibility of being wounded. Vulnerability feels raw and exposed. It makes one want to hide and protect oneself. Vulnerability can be societal or personal. I am not advocating that we accept societal vulnerability. This state can be dangerous. There are always people out there who will take advantage of vulnerable populations (women, children, non-whites, LBGTQ, immigrants). This kind of treatment of societal vulnerability is unacceptable. We must become aware of this predatory behavior where it exists, and work to make all people feel welcome and accepted.

Personal vulnerability, however, is part of everyone's existence. We all have parts of ourselves that we don't like or are ashamed of. How we deal with this reality is the key. When we start hiding those parts of ourselves that we consider flaws so that others won't notice, we are in effect cutting out part of our true self. When we define vulnerabilities as weaknesses, we give in to toxic shame. Then we fail to contribute our gifts to the betterment of the world.

As I mentioned in an earlier chapter, toxic shame is the result of not embracing our vulnerability. It is the inner sense of feeling flawed or insufficient as a person and believing that everyone can see it. The person feels like an oddity, and therefore exposed and vulnerable. Shame is often confused with guilt, but they are quite different. Guilt is about **doing** something wrong; shame is about **being** wrong. With guilt one can make amends, and there is hope. With shame there seems to be no solution except hiding oneself. With toxic shame, exposure is what is most feared. The antidote to this toxic shame is to come out of hiding, to let yourself be open, to encounter people who can mirror the good in you, who respond to you as a person and treat you with compassion. It is to recognize your own gifts and to see your vulnerabilities as part of who you are. It is to experience God loving you as you are.

> *"I went to therapy in order to reclaim my life."* (Carl)

For me, I started on the path to healing from toxic shame when I became aware that I didn't want to feel bad about myself any longer. I wanted to say "yes" to life, not just "no." So, I risked coming out of hiding. I began therapy and also delved into self-help books which dealt with shame. I explored how theology and psychology often contribute to shame, and that there are alternative ways of looking at things. All in all, it felt like a sacred journey. I was reclaiming my own goodness. As Mark Nepo says, "Ultimately it is where we are **not** perfect – where we are broken and cracked, where the wind whistles through – that is the stuff of transformation." (Nepo, October 18)

Healing from shame in order to reclaim our full selves is a lifelong journey. It takes a conversion of heart – coming to believe and accept that God has gifted all people with a basic goodness. It involves experiencing mirroring and responsiveness from my environment. It involves learning to accept and love all parts of oneself. And it involves sharing my vulnerabilities with others, as well as my strengths. Only then can I really *cheer lead* for others.

Surprisingly, I learned through this sharing of my vulnerabilities that I could truly be humble in a healthy way. Humility is not about hiding myself or being downtrodden, gloomy, or reticent. Actually, the word "humble" comes from "humus" or "earth". It means down-to-earth, comfortable in our skin, knowing our gifts, and bringing the fullness of who we are to everything we do. It implies being real, transparent, and unpretentious. It sometimes means having to say, "I'm sorry" or "I was wrong." It sometimes means "I don't have the skills to do this, but you do." And it could be as simple as saying "Thank you" when someone compliments you.

Sharing vulnerability fosters relationships. When I can share both my gifts **and** my vulnerabilities, others feel a connection to me, since they, too, have strengths and vulnerabilities. I modeled sharing my vulnerability in a healthy way when I wrote this to our sisters in our monthly newsletter:

> "I have been feeling a bit down lately… As always, God picks these times of vulnerability and weakness to enter more deeply into our lives. I sensed that divine opening within me this morning.… In that moment God showed me how my individual feelings and experiences are often a mirror of larger reality. We all experience vulnerability and shame at times. Our sharing of this experience can bring hope to others. Our contribution from the depth of our vulnerability and pain can move all of us toward a greater consciousness of unity." ("Reflections," October 2016)

If I as a *cheer leader* can show up with my whole self, with my gifts and my vulnerabilities, you might feel understood, connected, and inspired. It could lead you to want to share yourself as you are. And that will be the gift of leadership. As the back cover of Brené Brown's book, *I Thought It Was Just Me (But It Isn't)*, declares: "Our imperfections are what connect us to one another and to our humanity. Our vulnerabilities are not weaknesses; they are powerful reminders to keep our hearts and minds open to the reality that we're all in this together."

St. Oscar Romero was a true *cheer leader* for justice. When he first began his ministry as a priest in El Salvador, he didn't really notice the suffering of the poor. He even allied himself with the government and the military and closed his eyes to oppression. He protected himself so he didn't have to address the issues of injustice. But soon after becoming a bishop, he experienced a conversion. He began to really see and hear his people. He was haunted by the poverty, injustice, and violence that he saw all around him. He responded by becoming the voice of the poor in his life, his homilies, and his radio programs. He spoke truth to power. But the longer this went on, the more the powerful noticed him and warned him off of this dangerous path. Romero became more and more vulnerable. He received numerous death threats. But he chose to accept his vulnerability because he loved his people and he wanted to make their lives better. He said, "I do not believe in death without resurrection. If they kill me, I will rise again in the people of El Salvador." He was assassinated as he was saying Mass on March 24, 1980. St. Oscar Romero gave his whole being to bring truth and justice to the world. He dared to show up.

> *"During the COVID-19 pandemic, I wrote a vulnerable online piece about how I was trying to cope and what I was learning".*
> (Jerry)

"Showing up" as a leader implies risk. When people hear the word "risk," they often shudder. Risk involves great vulnerability, and this reality feels too dangerous for many people. They get scared. Inviting others to take risks is a daunting task for leaders. But for your mission to be accomplished, if it's worthwhile, means embracing all that serving the mission entails.

In preparing for our 2013 FSPA General Assembly entitled "Risk Boldly the Future," the planning team faced the task of helping the sisters to transition into new ways of living religious life. That meant letting go of institutions and ways of doing things that were tried and true, but which no longer helped us serve the needs of the 21st century. Addressing the need to take risks is risky (literally), but with an older crowd like we had, it seemed even harder. What the team did was plan small group sharing sessions for all the sisters where they were asked to tell stories of times when they and the FSPA community had taken huge risks. As they did this, we could see them sit taller in their chairs. Suddenly, risk didn't seem so scary anymore. This cheer now found resonance with them:

"We can do this, yes, we can;

We've done it before, and we can do it again."

Leaders are called to risk showing up, letting ourselves be seen, and using ourselves to make the world a better place. It won't always be easy, but it will be what we are called to do. When we show up as ourselves, vulnerable and gifted, our followers will be more likely to follow us, because they recognize one like themselves. Being vulnerable with people establishes community. And together we can create new life.

REFLECTION QUESTIONS

- Name 3 gifts that you have and 3 vulnerabilities. Can you accept all of them?

- Remember a time when you were able to embrace a personal vulnerability and use that occasion to connect with others. What was the result?

- Where have you risked showing up as a leader to make the world a better place?

7

CLAIMING OUR VOICE

One requisite for being a cheerleader is having the ability to shout, to use one's voice loudly enough to be heard and grab attention. Our cheerleading squad did just that.

"We are the New Hawks, we couldn't be prouder,

If you can't hear us now, we'll yell a little louder!"

(repeat more loudly each time)

But, ironically, claiming my voice in the rest of my life has been one of the hardest things I've ever had to do. And fittingly, this chapter was also one of the most difficult to write. Maybe it's because I am a woman and the world has told women over and over again to be quiet, that we have no voice. And, unfortunately, we have often believed it. Or maybe, just maybe, claiming our voice is simply one of the most important and arduous journeys that we as human beings can and need to undertake. In essence, claiming our voice is proclaiming who we really are at our core and why we are on this earth. St. Catherine of Siena stated: "If you are what you should be, you will set the whole world ablaze." That's a pretty powerful statement!

Voice (as I am using the term) is the expression of who we are created to be. It comes from deep within and is unique to each person, since each of us is created with gifts given only to us to help create a better world. And our voice wants to be expressed. Carly Fleischmann, a young woman with autism who has never been able to speak but learned to express her inner voice through typing, wrote this in *Carly's Voice*:

> "So, why do I call my voice my 'inner voice'? The truth is ever since I was a young child, I talked. The words never flowed out of my mouth or came out of my head to be shared with the outside world, but I talked to myself in my head....
>
> So, as you can see, I always had a voice. It was just inside me.... My voice was always special to me even though it was only for me to hear... I do believe we all have an inner voice and it's just trying to find its way out." (Fleischmann, pp. 360-361)

We are each born unique and full of possibilities. As we grow and learn, we develop our gifts (some more than others) and gradually claim them. But sometimes we lose a sense of our uniqueness in order to fit into the culture. We may learn to be "good" boys and girls, rigidly following rules, trying to make others happy at the expense of ourselves. We may learn that we are not okay according to society's standards. We may learn that to get ahead, we have to become like others.

This is admittedly all part of learning to fit into a culture, but it shouldn't be at the expense of one's true self. Unless we have parents, teachers, and friends who are *cheer leaders* for who we really are, we begin to give in to the "shoulds" and squelch the unique parts of ourselves which are vital for our contribution to the world. As author Susan Forward stated:

> "No matter how confused, self-doubting, or ambivalent we are about what's happening in our interactions with other people, we can never entirely silence the inner voice that always tells us the truth. We may not like the sound of the truth, and we often let it murmur just outside our consciousness, not stopping long enough to listen. But when we pay attention to it, it leads us toward wisdom, health, and clarity. That voice is the guardian of our integrity." (Forward and Frazier)

It took me many years to trust God and myself enough to claim and to speak what was deep within me. One major turning point for me happened as I was sitting in my therapist's office. He was listening very attentively, as usual, but not saying much, also as usual. I was going around and around in an endless loop of questioning what I was going to do about something or other. Finally, irritated with him for not helping me and feeling desperate, I confronted him, "Why don't you just tell me what to do?" He calmly replied, "How can I tell you what to do? I'm not you. The answer is within you." I don't think it hit me right away. But he was cheering for me. The impact of his words has stayed with me all these years. Deep down I have an inner voice, and I can trust it.

The next step is to communicate using your inner voice. It takes effort and practice, but it's very important. Recently I saw the movie *Poms* for the third time. (I guess once a cheerleader, always a cheerleader.) What impressed me most about the film was how the older women featured in it had always wanted to express their inner voice, but

> "Recently I had the courage to respectfully tell my mother that I didn't agree with her."
> (Lashonda)

for some reason were not allowed to do so. However, when they had the chance to form a cheerleading squad, they took to it enthusiastically no matter what other people said. They found their inner voice and shouted it to the world. Never would they let go of it again. What an inspiring story and what a lesson!

Expressing our true inner voice always speaks the good; otherwise it can't be from God. Some people seem to think that hiding in a crowd and chanting hate speech is an act of claiming their inner voice. However, what it really is is cowardice. It is tapping into the emotional frenzy of a group which is directed negatively toward others. To truly claim my inner voice I must use "I" language and communicate feelings and thoughts that express yearning for the common good. It is about honoring both myself and the other. In therapeutic work, we teach people to use this formula: "I feel *(emotion)* because *(reason)*, and I wish *(possible solution)*." An example of this might be the following: "I feel angry because immigrants are being targeted, and I wish that we could realize that we are all immigrants." Another example might be this: "I feel scared because my wages can't support my family, and I wish that we could all work together to solve wage disparity."

Speaking my wisdom is scary, and sometimes it feels like one is not being heard. But it's important to be faithful to it. My inner voice was too important, and I owe it to myself and others to communicate it. If I don't contribute my two cents worth to the discussion, something will be missing, and everyone will suffer. I took to heart this passage from the Hebrew Scripture:

> "The word of the Lord came to me: Before I formed you in the womb I knew you, before you were born I dedicated you, a prophet to the nations I appointed you. 'Ah, Lord God!' I said, 'I do not know how to speak. I am too young!' But the Lord answered me, 'Do not say, 'I am too young.' To whomever I send you, you shall go; whatever I command you, you shall speak. Do not be afraid of them, for I am with you to deliver you." (Jeremiah 1:4-8 NAB)

Rosa Parks, on that December day in 1955 in Montgomery, Alabama, would never have thought of herself as a prophet to the world. She had long been involved as an organizer in the Civil Rights Movement. But on that day, she was just tired. Not tired physically, but tired of the lack of respect for her as a person and the lack of equality for her African American people. As Parks herself said, "I was tired of giving in." So instead of going to the back of the segregated bus, she sat in a front seat. When the bus driver told her to move to the back, she refused. Parks was jailed but didn't give up. She became one of the lead planners and organizers of the Montgomery Bus Boycott. This resistance movement eventually led to the integration of public transportation in Montgomery. Parks continued her work against

> *"At a committee meeting I voiced a minority viewpoint even though I knew it would meet with resistance."*
> *(Keri)*

racial discrimination and injustice throughout her long life. She was awarded the Presidential Medal of Freedom and the Congressional Gold Medal for her efforts. Rosa Parks truly claimed her voice as a prophet to the world.

A prophet speaks truth to power. In my experience, I have been inspired by our own FSPA prophet, Sister Thea Bowman. In the 1970s and 1980s, Sister Thea Bowman, FSPA, became a national leader and advocate for Black Catholics. She was fearless. Through her passionate speaking and singing, she was a "prophetic witness to the eradication of racism" in the church. (Fr. Maurice Nutt) She even managed to get the U.S Catholic bishops at their semi-annual meeting to stand together and sing "We Shall Overcome." Now that took guts! Thea used her voice to make a powerful difference. Today she is being considered for sainthood because she found good in the world and proclaimed it to the rooftops.

Like Rosa Parks and Thea Bowman, once we have claimed our inner voice, the universe is calling us to share it more widely. Again, from the Hebrew Scripture: "The Lord God has given me a well-trained tongue, that I might know how to speak to the weary a word that will rouse them." (Isaiah 50:4NAB) We have a duty as humans to share our small piece of wisdom with our fellow travelers on this earth.

We as sisters also needed to claim our collective voice, but in a new way that would speak to the needs of people in the 21st century. As Joan Chittister, OSB, challenged women religious in 2006, "We must be those who live at the center of society to leaven it, at the bottom of society to speak for it, and on the edge of society to critique it." (LCWR address, 2006) In the past, sisters did this by being leaders in many church arenas. The Catholic healthcare and educational systems in the U.S. are a testament to their excellent leadership skills.

Sisters have been fierce in addressing the needs of the poor, the outcast, and the immigrant. But as the needs of the world changed, sisters changed with them. Now sisters are using their collective voices as lobbyists for Catholic social teaching, as social service workers, as retreat and spirituality center directors. They are collaborating with others to address homelessness and human trafficking, promoting care for the earth, organizing ministry to Hispanics, and tending to the migrants. Leadership no longer entails just being the head person or CEO. Now it also means embracing our roles as initiators, collaborators, inspirers, conveners, and participants with other mission-driven people in the larger community wherever we are needed.

We all have a call as *cheer leaders* to "hear each other into speech." (Nelle Morton) This refers especially to those on the margins who are seen as not having a voice. Some of us can access and connect with power in ways that the poor may not be able to. But in our interactions, we need to always remember that their voices are just as important as ours. Like my therapist said, we don't know their unique wisdom until they tell us. As Joan Chittister says in her book, *The Time is Now: The Call to Uncommon Courage*:

> "It is now our task, as individuals, as intentional groups, wherever we are on the social spectrum, to shine our light on the lives [of those on the margins].... It is the task of each of us to be their voice until they can be heard themselves. It is the individual prophet's task, whatever we do and wherever we are, to point out their absence in society, their needs, the inequities they bear. It is our task to give them hope, to give them possibility, to help the outcasts to fit in." (Chittister, p. 103)

However, we can't stop there. A big part of our task as *cheer leaders* is to encourage others to speak their wisdom. Two small examples illustrate this adage. A group of executives sat around a table planning a renovation. The question for the committee that particular day was what kind of carpet would be the best. They kept tossing around suggestions until one wise member said, "Shouldn't we have housekeepers and maintenance people on this committee? They're the ones who will be dealing with the carpet every day; they surely know more than we do." Another example was told by a man who installs billboards. He reported, "Too often, company executives and ad designers create the billboards at their desks. When I get the billboard to install, the public can't read it. The text is too small. I could have told them that there's a big difference between seeing a billboard on a computer and seeing one from your car as you drive along." The lesson is this: we need to hear the voices of everyone who has a stake in an issue and invite them to speak.

Woodrow Wilson said, "The ear of the leader must ring with the voices of the people." That's what a true *cheer leader* does – listens deeply, hears the people, and then uses his or her skills to invite others to share their wisdom and insight. This can happen in many different situations, from the streets to family dinner tables to corporate board rooms. If we do encourage everyone to share, we will certainly encounter rich diversity. Not everybody will agree, and many times there will be strong feelings on all sides. It can get messy. But if we can truly believe that everyone has a piece of the truth, we will want to hear everyone because otherwise something will be missing.

If you have embraced your call to leadership, your story is probably not much different than mine. It's a risky venture to put ourselves out there with our truth. Believe me, I understand. But nothing less is asked of us. We need to risk speaking our voice and hearing the voice of others. Together we need to embrace this call: "Be not a whisper that is lost in the wind; be a voice that is heard above the storms of life." (Maimonides)

REFLECTION QUESTIONS

- Can you remember a time when you actually recognized your inner voice? Describe the scene.

- Name a person who encouraged you to speak your voice in public. What was the situation? What happened and how did you feel about it?

- Remember a time when you became a "voice for the voiceless" until they could claim their own voice.

8
SEEING INTO BEING

She was wandering around the room, touching things, glancing at cartoon characters on the TV, sometimes laughing to herself. This went on for many minutes. I looked at her the whole time. She noticed me but avoided looking at me. At one point she rubbed her eyes with the back of her fists. I copied her movements while looking at her intently. She noticed but immediately turned away. After more wandering, she again rubbed her eyes with her fists, and I did the same. She noticed my copying of her movements, and this time she smiled. She went back to wandering and touching, gradually moving closer to me. After a while, she came right up to me, looked intently at me, and, with her fists on her eyes, and my fists on my eyes, she leaned into me so that we were connected, fist to fist, eye to eye. We gazed deeply at each other for five seconds or so. Then she left me and resumed her wandering.

This girl is my little friend with autism. She is non-verbal, but, nevertheless, in this instance she and I communicated at a very deep level. Parents recognize this kind of connection.

They have gazed deeply into the eyes of their baby, and their infant has gazed back at them in a sacred moment of connection.

This is cheering for the other in its deepest sense. We are saying to the person, often non-verbally, "You are special. You are beloved. I'm glad you are here." As Richard Rohr states, "It appears that humans only know themselves through the gaze of others." When we gaze into each other's eyes, we detect blessing or curse, inclusion or indifference, welcome or rejection.

> *"I write to a prisoner once a month to provide hope and connection."*
> (Jason)

When I was a cheerleader, I made sure I looked intently at the individuals in the crowd. I needed to connect with them and tap into their wavelength. I let them know that they and the team were valuable, that I appreciated them, and that we needed each other.

"Two, four, six, eight,

Who do we appreciate?

New Hawks! New Hawks! New Hawks!"

Connecting deeply with one another creates a movement of mutual openness, trust, goodness. In that environment, people want to work together. The *cheer leader* is uniquely equipped and ready to see the whole group into being, creating a powerful energy for mission. However, at times there are individuals in the group who can't seem to open themselves to the positive energy of the group. They may see the world as negative or cling to a worldview of "us vs. them". In these cases, the leader needs to address the issue with the group. He or she might say something like this: "We're all working on the same mission. Haven't we all committed to it? Everyone in the group has something valuable to contribute, and we need everyone's contributions. We depend on each other. We are in this together."

> "I volunteer at the YWCA, empowering young women to claim their goodness and strengths." (Pamela)

A *cheer leader* is called to connect with all of the followers, to demonstrate to them that they are all valued and respected. He/she becomes an instrument for igniting each person's God-given life and energy for good. This is especially important when the followers are suffering or feeling unworthy. At times like these, people will often turn away to protect themselves. To look one another in the eye is to reveal one's inner self, and this may seem too painful or vulnerable. Real connection may involve empathizing with the suffering person to the point of tears. As St. Oscar Romero said, "There are many things that can only be seen through eyes that have cried."

In the Christian Scriptures, Jesus often showed himself to be a *cheer leader*. The healing that he accomplished involved helping others to reclaim their own dignity and worth. To Zaccheus, a hated tax collector and sinner, Jesus showed respect and said, "Come down [from the tree]. Today I go to your house." He asked the man born lame, "Do you want to walk?" When the man replied, "Yes," Jesus said, "Get up, take your mat, and walk." Jesus recognized the courage and potential in the man and encouraged him.

One of my favorite Scripture stories is the story of Jesus and the woman with a hemorrhage. This unnamed woman had suffered from a bleeding disorder for twelve years.

She had tried in vain to find healing and relief, but no one could help her. To make matters worse, according to Jewish law at that time, bleeding was considered a sign of impurity. Anyone who was bleeding, most notably women who were menstruating, were not allowed to touch anyone or anything that was considered ritually clean. They were isolated during that time. The woman in the story had endured isolation and shunning for too long. When she heard of Jesus' compassion and healing power, she courageously decided to simply touch his cloak, hoping she could be healed in that connection. Maybe he wouldn't even notice. But he did notice. Instead of banning her, he looked into her eyes with compassion and she was healed. "Daughter, your faith has made you well; go in peace." (Luke 8:48 NRSV)

Diarmuid O'Murchu interprets the story this way:

"If words were spoken by Jesus, [this might be the gist]: 'Even though you are a woman with an unfortunate bleeding condition, you are nonetheless a full person before God and before the world. Rise above your plight and get on with your life.' It is not some miraculous words that seal the miracle; it is the *compassionate gaze as the core ingredient of [this] encounter.*" (O'Murchu, p. 158)

St. Clare of Assisi, a partner of St. Francis in initiating Franciscan spirituality, also knew the importance of "seeing into being." Visual prayer for her involved looking deeply at an image of Christ, connecting with the person of Jesus, and gradually being led to transformation into a true disciple of the Good News to the world. Clare's method of visual prayer is composed of four movements:

- **Gaze** – fix your eyes on the Christ image. (This can be anything in creation which reveals God to you.)
- **Consider** – involve your mind and imagination. How does this image speak to you of God? Do you sense a call to transformation?
- **Contemplate** – be still and let God speak to you.
- **Imitate** – thank God and take what God has inspired in you out into the world.

As Ronald Rolheiser states: "In the gaze of true recognition there is a deep blessing." (Rolheiser, p. 223) Embrace it and go forth to serve the world.

Pope Francis has been urging all the world's people to engage in a "culture of encounter." What he calls "encuentro" is not just meeting people on a superficial level, a "Hi, how are you?" type of thing. To Francis, "encuentro" means a deep looking at and listening to people and all of creation, appreciating oneself and the other as true gifts of God, and being transformed by the encounter. It is what *cheer leaders* do when they're at their best.

Chris, a woman I know, told me the story recently of when she truly encountered and cheered for creation. She was in the house painting and happened to look outside. What she saw horrified her. The city works department was starting to cut down one of only two trees left on her boulevard. Still in her paint clothes, she ran down to the city works department and demanded that they cease cutting down the tree. They said their hands were tied; she needed to talk with the mayor. So, she did. She went to his office immediately, paint clothes and all. The mayor listened and agreed to put the issue on the upcoming council meeting agenda. It was agreed that they would leave the tree standing. Overjoyed and humbled, Chris and a friend wrapped the tree in order to heal its cuts, and then prayed a blessing prayer over it. Energy flowed between them, and both tree and humans were transformed. True *encuentro*!!

Jadav Payeng is another example of *encuentro* between human and nature. Payeng is known as the "forest man of India." He saw how increased flooding had changed the flow of the Brahmaputra River in his home state of Assam and created an island of sandbars where no vegetation could survive. The land that had once been rich with numerous plants, trees, and animals was now a barren wasteland. So, nearly forty years ago, he began to plant trees. He described his actions for the environment in a radio interview on National Public Radio:

> "First with bamboo trees, then with cotton trees. I kept planting – all different kinds of trees. It's not as if I did it alone. You plant one or two trees, and they have to seed. And once they seed, the wind knows how to plant them, the birds here know how to sow them, cows know, elephants know, even the river knows. The entire ecosystem knows." (McCarthy, December 26, 2017)

Now the island is filled with tall grass and thousands of trees, populated by tigers, deer, monkeys, elephants, and a variety of birds. Through his one simple action, Payeng became a *cheer leader* for nature, encouraging it to do what it knows how to do best.

Cheer leaders create movements for good by truly encountering "the other." Cynthia Bourgeault puts it this way:

"The Kingdom of Heaven is the enlightened radiance of the eye that looks straight into being and sees that it is the Body of Christ – each bird, leaf, tree, the fullness of Being hidden in the random dots of the universe, totally transparent to the love that is its source and its destiny. Meaning dances with meaning; our human lives are set ablaze to release the root energy of love, and we discover to our amazement just how much love can be borne in human flesh." (Bourgeault, p.181).

Let us gaze upon all creation so deeply that this encounter transforms us. Together may we see each other into being.

REFLECTION QUESTIONS

- What does "seeing into being" mean to you?

- Have you had a true "encuentro" lately? Describe it. How did you feel afterward?

- How can you help people to heal through graced encounters?

9

USING POWER TO MAKE A DIFFERENCE

I don't know if I've ever felt as powerful as I did when I was a cheerleader. We had the total attention of the whole crowd, and when we started the cheer, all the disparate people in the throng followed us and shouted as one, animating and carrying the spirit of the team. I can remember the gym shaking as we all clapped, stomped, and cheered:

"[Clap, clap, stomp, Clap, clap, stomp!]

(Repeat 2 x)

We will, we will, rock you!!"

(Repeat)

Leaders are powerful people! Actually, we're all powerful people, and we all can be leaders. Do these statements make you cringe? When I first tell people, especially women, that we all are powerful, many of them don't want to hear it. They often deflect by responding like this: "Thinking one is powerful is very egotistical;" or "Powerful people are dangerous;" or "Maybe 'strong' would be a better word than 'powerful'." Mind you, this feedback is coming from women who have been leaders throughout their lives. What these statements do is reflect the millennia-old mores given to women: be subservient, don't congratulate yourself, stay at home, know your place. Sometimes the only route left to women has been indirect leadership or even passive-aggressive actions.

I can identify with the hesitancy of these women to claim their power. I felt the same way for half my life, and sometimes still do. Brené Brown, the social worker, researcher, and writer on shame and vulnerability, in her numerous interviews with women, found this pattern to be very common. She says, "Power is a difficult topic for women. The majority of women I talk to are uncomfortable with the idea of a 'powerful woman.'" (Brown, *I Thought It Was Just Me (But It Isn't)*, p. 23)

There are many reasons for this, both societal and religious. For many millennia, women around the world have lacked significant power in society, government, and religion. They were seen as less than men, physically, intellectually, emotionally, and even morally (remember Eve.) Noted theologians like St. Thomas Aquinas described "the nature of females as being defective and misbegotten." Even today, when women exert their power, they can often expect responses ranging from harsh or demeaning criticism to actual violence. Women have learned to keep their power hidden, or they shared it in a group where the group was seen as wielding the power.

Men, too, have their own issues with power. Like women, they often have expectations put upon them by society which keep them in a box. But the expectations are different. Brené Brown, after interviewing men, found that the major expectation they deal with is "Do not let people see anything that can be perceived as weakness." (Brown, *I Thought ...*, p. 280) So, claiming power for men often involves repressing feelings, denying vulnerability, earning a lot of money, putting everyone in their place, and climbing their way to the top or die trying. (Brown, *Daring Greatly*, p. 107)

As you can see, the concept of real and honest power seems to be a hard one to grasp. It has accrued centuries of mistaken interpretation, and has often crippled people. Countries, also, seem to think that they need to demonstrate their power by bullying smaller countries, threatening military might rather than truly negotiating, and protecting themselves at the cost of the common good. Presidential candidates, too, tout their all-knowing and rigid positions because they don't want their constituents to think they are weak. Brown calls this behavior "power-over":

> "Unfortunately, when most of us hear the word 'power' we automatically jump to the concept of power-over – the idea that power is the ability to control people, take advantage of others or exert force over somebody or something. We think of power as finite – there's only so much, so if I'm going to get some, I'm forced to take it away from you. Power-over is a dangerous form of power." (Brown, *I Thought It Was ...*, p. 24)

Granted, there are times when a leader needs to exert control, mainly in emergencies. But, even in those situations, the leader should gather a group around him or her to give wise advice. Decisions should be made through listening and collaborating. Using power-over constantly and as the norm without respect for the gifts and dignity of others is not the type of power that we want to see in our leaders. It destroys people rather than building them up. It creates divisions and resentment. We have seen too much of that kind of power used by leaders lately.

> "As a mother of young children, I ran for the school board in order to bring my experience of discovering the potential in children." (Kelsey)

It is important for leaders to embrace their "real power." Brown describes "real power" thus:

> "[Real power] is the ability to make change happen. Real power is unlimited – we don't need to fight over it because there is plenty to go around.... It's something we create and build with others." (Brown, *I Thought It Was ...*, p.25)

Mary Parker Follett, a social worker, author, and business consultant in the late 19th and early 20th centuries, adds another nuance. She advocated for "power with" which she describes as "at once relational and collective. It creates new possibilities from the very differences that might exist in the group." (Briskin, Erickson, Ott, and Callanan, p. 94)

This kind of relational power is needed by leaders today to build strong teams and movements. This is the kind of power that grows as it touches more people. It is based on deep listening and a willingness to stay at the table and work together with others on mutual solutions for as long as is needed. This is the kind of power which makes leaders effective and someone the group can rally around.

A significant example of this type of group power emerged in 2009 when the Leadership Conference of Women Religious (LCWR) was informed by the Vatican that it had grave concerns about the leadership and orthodoxy of the conference. (To see a fuller explanation of the situation, I suggest the excellent book *However Long the Night: Making Meaning in a Time of Crisis*, Annmarie Sanders, IHM, ed.) This pronouncement provoked shock, anger, and sadness among LCWR members and their many supporters around the country. People wanted them to fight back publicly, to use their power in a dominating and accusatory way. But the leaders and members of LCWR chose to engage in a process of using power in a way that healed rather than divided.

A brief overview of the process reveals the elements important in using power in a way that brings people together. First of all, the LCWR leadership, members, and their member congregations entered into contemplative prayer and discernment throughout the process, which led to a deep grounding in God. Also, from the beginning and throughout the process, the group offered members opportunities to surface, express, and process their strong emotions in a safe environment. These actions freed them up to engage in respectful dialogue with openness and integrity. In addition, reviewing and affirming the LCWR mission grounded them and provided clarity and strength. LCWR leaders, in their ongoing relationship with Vatican representatives, committed themselves to speaking truth, listening deeply, opening themselves to be transformed, and, at the same time, retaining the integrity of the organization. The leadership vowed to faithfully continue the dialogue for as long as it took. It took six years, and in the end, both sides and their relationship were transformed. This process has become a model for others in negotiating polarization, conflict, and misunderstanding through the grace of God with integrity and communion intact.

Power doesn't always mean being out in the forefront. Sometimes power consists in building trust as a person or organization which does the right thing. Once trusting relationships have been built, power may involve tapping into that trust to invite others to gather to accomplish something good. Recently, when FSPA decided to fight human trafficking in our city, we didn't go at the task alone. We invited leaders from the city, non-profits, our affiliates, and other interested parties to address it together. Previously most of these groups had been working alone. But, because FSPA has power and respect in La Crosse, the groups came to the meetings and decided to work together with us. We wouldn't have had the expertise to do it alone. It was a beautiful thing to behold. Inviting everyone to the table increased the power for good exponentially.

Using our power takes great courage. It must be grounded in something bigger than ourselves because it's often such a long and challenging process. By ourselves we might give up and resort to discouragement and apathy. But God's promises to us provide the support we need: "My love and grace are enough for you," and "God can do infinitely more than we can ask or imagine."

FSPA relies deeply on God for our power, manifested in one way through its practice of Perpetual Adoration. We call our Perpetual Adoration chapel our "powerhouse." There, sisters (and now united with our prayer partners) have consciously prayed daily for the

> "At the city council meeting, I suggested that we bring in a facilitator to help us make a decision in an extremely contentious environment." (Kevin)

world and its needs for over 140 years. Every year we respond to 30,000 prayer requests from over 130 different locations around the globe. What a great way to proclaim to the world where real power lies! The power of God's love for us and for the world is what propels us forward and gives our leadership the strength, energy, and wisdom to serve the community and the world.

In high school, when our team, cheerleaders, and fans went to a basketball tournament, we were often vying for two trophies, one for the team for winning the tournament, and the other for best sportsmanship of a team's players, cheerleaders, and fans. This dual trophy presentation celebrated the fact that respect for others was just as important as winning a game. The good sportsmanship trophy was presented to the cheerleaders because it was our responsibility to steer the energy toward the good. This required us to embrace our power, often in the midst of a negative scenario. How everyone acted mattered. It wasn't always easy, but together we could do it.

When we know ourselves as gifted and decide to share that gift with others, we are using our power to create the larger good. We are making an impact on our environment. *Cheer leaders* definitely make an impact. They use their abilities to motivate the crowd to claim and express their power. United power, as you know, can literally shake the rafters. As Margaret Mead said, "Never doubt that a small group of thoughtful committed citizens can change the world. Indeed, it is the only thing that ever has."

In order to change the world, we all need to claim our power, individual and collective. I love this passage by Marianne Williamson from her book *Return to Love*. It reminds us that we are not serving ourselves or anyone else if we deny our power.

"Our deepest fear is not that we are inadequate. Our deepest fear is that we are powerful beyond measure. It is our light, not our darkness, that frightens us. We ask ourselves, 'Who am I to be brilliant, gorgeous, talented, and fabulous?' Actually, who are you not to be? You are a child of God. Your playing small doesn't serve the world. There's nothing enlightened about shrinking so that other people won't feel insecure around you. We are all meant to shine, as children do. We were born to make manifest the glory of God that is within us. It's not just in some of us; it's in everyone. And as we let our own light shine, we unconsciously give other people permission to do the same. As we are liberated from our own fear, our presence automatically liberates others." (Marianne Williamson)

Reflection Questions
- Do you consider yourself "powerful?" How does power manifest itself in you?

- Ponder one line from Marianne Williamson's quote that really speaks to you.

- How can you use power effectively as a *cheer leader*?

10

COMMUNICATING THE MISSION

Good cheerleading is based on good communication. It's all about conveying the real and the immediate in a way that fans can understand. It's best when it is rooted in the familiar and touches deeply held desires and values. Through presence, words, and actions we help our fans elevate our team to victory.

But this scenario is too often far from the communication we receive from our leaders in the world today. Fake news! Post-truth! Toxic dialogue! These warped communications twist the truth and deceive people for the benefit of the powerful. Nobody knows what to believe anymore. This is especially problematic for leaders since communication is one of the most important skills of leadership. As PR specialist and author James Hoggan bemoans,

> "We are in a communication crisis. Our warlike approach to public debate is polluting the public square with a dark haze of unyielding one-sidedness.

Regardless of the issue, this is the threshold problem because we have shut down the space where high quality public debate takes place, where facts matter, where passionate opposition and science shape constructive, mind changing conversations." (Hoggan, "Speak the Truth, but Not to Punish")

We hunger for direct and real communication which builds trust and relationship, even when we disagree. We want to be inspired to action for the good. We thirst for a sense of oneness with the rest of the world, feeling its joys and pains as our own. But this type of communication is more and more rare. This is one of the reasons I chose to write this book. I want people to seek and communicate the truth, their own and others, based on deep values, transparency, and trust. How else can we grow as a people?

When I became the leader of my congregation, I chose to address issues up front and be transparent with my sisters and the public. I tried to listen and be open to what they thought and felt, so that our team could better serve their needs. This built trust and a new awareness of the need for deep dialogue and the value of everyone's wisdom. We as a community practiced "contemplative dialogue" which begins with a period of silence where each person can tap into the Spirit of God, something larger than themselves. Then everyone in the circle has an opportunity to share and be listened to without interruption. Next, back and forth communication hopefully deepens understanding. And finally there is a period of thanksgiving for the willingness of all to share their vulnerability and become more deeply united.

Good communication can make all the difference. By how things are worded and proclaimed, listeners may be outraged or inspired by the same event. One close-to-home example of the need for expert communication took place when FSPA decided to hand over governance of our sponsored institutions to their lay leaders in 2017. (There is a description of this event in chapter 4.) This was a decision that needed to be communicated well to our affiliates, employees, partners in mission, donors, and the general public because many people had a vested interest in our sponsored ministries. We had sponsored these publicly-incorporated ministries for over 100 years and they had become the face of FSPA in many sectors. How could we accomplish this transition in a way that spoke to people of our integrity and our ongoing commitment to mission and ministry, but in a new way? Here is part of the official announcement we crafted for the news release in November 2017:

> "La Crosse, Wisconsin—Since 1849, the Franciscan Sisters of Perpetual Adoration have served in areas of greatest need. In its early years, that meant establishing health care and addressing education needs, ultimately leading to the creation of what are now [2 Catholic hospitals and a university], organizations that are firmly established and thriving through the day-to-day care of lay partners.
>
> In order to remain true to its calling to address the evolving needs of humankind, FSPA today announced it intends to transfer complete oversight of those organizations to lay leaders for each organization. This action removes FSPA from sponsorship of the ministries allowing it to more fully focus on people on the margins of society."

Because this communication rang true to our mission and who we are, and at the same time displayed honesty, forthrightness, and inspiration, the public understood. Instead of an uproar of fear or anger, what we received from people instead was sadness over the change, but also understanding and gratitude for the service we had provided and inspiration for the years to come.

> "When I go on Facebook, I challenge posts that I know to be untrue or inflammatory."
> (Doug)

But there are still times when as leaders we face negative attacks on us or our movement or organization. The natural reaction is to want to lash out, to set the attacker straight, and get back at them at the same time. It's so tempting. But as *cheer leaders* we lose our effectiveness if we let our energy spew out indiscriminately. We need to harness that energy, tap in again to the mission, and then craft a message which speaks the truth. Many times I needed help with this because of my own deep emotions. Jane, our FSPA Director of Communications, was invaluable in these instances. She often had to "talk me down," and only then were we able to respond with openness, integrity, and inspiration. My advice – find someone like Jane. We all need help communicating in difficult times.

Great communicators also adapt to the style of the times in order to better connect with the people. Noted historian and biographer, Doris Kearns Goodwin, in her interview on "How to Lead" on CNN, illustrated this. She revealed that Abraham Lincoln relied on powerful speeches, while, in addition to speeches, Teddy Roosevelt used the power of newspapers to communicate his message. Franklin Roosevelt came into people's homes with his "fireside chats" on the radio, while John F. Kennedy and Ronald Reagan communicated powerfully on television. Our recent presidents have used social media as one way to communicate their messages.

> "When racial discrimination happened in our city, I got a group together to learn more about white privilege so we could address the issue." (George)

Unfortunately, the internet and social media, while making information easier to get, have also encouraged people to make everything all about them, from Facebook to Twitter. How one feels personally has often been substituted for actual facts. As long as you say something often enough, people will begin to believe you, with no proof that what you are saying is actually based in truth. And when government leaders start to "govern by tweet," so-called official communication devolves to the status of no more than individual opinions. What happened to an emphasis on the common good?

Sometimes the most effective communication is not only in words, but in words and actions. Pope Francis uniquely proclaimed who he was on the day of his election. When he was first presented to the people as the new pope in 2013, he wanted the crowd to know that he was one of them. The images he created proclaimed that message loud and clear. When he came out on the balcony, he was attired in a simple white cassock, rather than the imperial robes worn by previous popes. Instead of using a platform to elevate himself above the cardinals standing with him, as had been the tradition, he remained at the same level. And most astounding to the people was the fact that before Pope Francis gave them his blessing, he asked them to pray for him. This had never been done before. All the images proclaimed who he was to the world, a humble man of the people.

At other times humor is what is needed to break down barriers and change stereotypes better than ordinary serious communication. Remember, the word "humor" comes from the same root as the word "humility." But, for some reason, humor is not often seen as a desirable quality in a leader. A number of writers have noted that Americans like humor but think that their leaders need to be serious. However, many times, humor is the only way to get the truth across to the people. The juxtaposition of reality with preposterousness surprises and engages people, pulling them up short and making them think. As Stephen Wilbers states,

> "Humor reduces the distance between writer and reader (and between speaker and listener). It makes readers and listeners pay attention, and it helps them remember what they've heard. Because of these attributes, it's a powerful tool, both in writing and in teaching." (Wilbers, p. 279)

One example of where I took advantage of this juxtaposition was a fundraiser for a local non-profit organization. The theme for the evening was "Game On" based on the format for a TV show called "Game Night" where contestants compete in hilarious tasks to gain points. FSPA has attended many fundraisers for worthy organizations through the years, but often they have tended to be more formal and serious affairs. Since this was going to be anything but formal, I wanted to communicate that sisters are like everyone else, ready for a fun time while at the same time helping others. So, after our team of four was introduced, we dropped to our knees with our hands folded and our eyes turned heavenward (a usual stereotype for sisters). It certainly got the audience's attention. (Actually, I learned later that the organizers of the event were horrified at that moment, thinking that we sisters were going to use the evening to proselytize.) Then I proceeded to pray:

> "Dear Lord, we pray for the other teams gathered here. We know that they are going to lose, so please give them hope that they could maybe win next time. They are good people and should hold their heads high.
>
> We also pray for our team. We know we will emerge victorious tonight, so please give us humility. May our heads not get too big, just because of our great talent and expertise. Thank you for your help. Amen."

The juxtaposition of our stance with our words surprised the crowd. By the end of our prayer they were laughing hysterically and rose to a standing ovation. A bit of humor was able to communicate our oneness, that we aren't so different. (Oh, by the way, we almost won but a team of doctors edged us out on the last trivia question, which just happened to be a science question. Strangely, there was no religion question to be found. Just saying...!)

On a more serious note, William Zinsser, in his book *On Writing Well*, said this about humor:

> "The columns that I wrote for *Life* made people laugh. But they had a serious purpose, which was to say: 'Something crazy is going on here – some erosion in the quality of life, or some threat to life itself, and yet everyone assumes it's normal.' Today the outlandish

becomes routine overnight. The humorist is trying to say that it's still outlandish." (Zinsser, p. 211)

Leaders often have the responsibility of waking their followers up to the reality of a situation. And one of the best ways is to do it through humor, but always a type of humor which is not snide or derisive but with which ordinary people can identify. That way people can understand it and feel connected. Humor balances the hard things in life. When experiencing division or painful events, humor can touch into negative feelings in a transformational way. Instead of feeling helpless with confusion, anger, fear, or anxiety, people are led to the truth of what's happening to them and come to feel grounded and empowered.

The 14th Dalai Lama of Tibet is one of the most skilled and prolific communicators and *cheer leaders* alive today. Although he is now in his mid-80s, he still has a vibrant social media presence (his own website and accounts with Twitter, Facebook, and Instagram.) He travels all over the world teaching and speaking on topics such as Tibetan liberation from China, Buddhism and science, peace and non-violence, and interfaith dialogue. He has also appeared in numerous films. But even with his serious and compelling message, what makes the Dalai Lama such an appealing figure is who he is and how he delivers his message. I attended one of his talks at a peace conference. He is this little rotund smiling man who seemed totally relaxed and at home with himself. He radiated peace and humility. And he constantly used humor to make his points, some of it self-deprecating and some of it lovingly chiding of the audience. I left that day loving him and feeling energized and inspired to be a better person. That's what a *cheer leader* can do.

In my own leadership journey, I used humor a lot, sometimes in a self-deprecating manner, sometimes to make a point. I found that using humor helped the people I was addressing to identify with me and better understand my point. And they often remembered more clearly the points I made through humor than the ones delivered when I was overly serious. Once I wore a pair of Martian antennae to a community meeting to convey our need as a community to embrace "Planet Future." The sisters got the message. Incongruous portrayals like this one seemed to find a unique niche in their memories, making it easier to recall the message and have it inform their lives.

Cheer leaders must take great care with their communications. What they say must be true to who they are, and at the same time provide inspiration and hope to their followers. I remember this cheer from high school; it was a great cheer to communicate who we were and what our mission was:

> "Everywhere we go, people want to know,
>
> Who we are, so we tell them,
>
> We are the New Hawks, mighty, mighty New Hawks!
>
> Go, fight, win!"

We all felt empowered and inspired to bring about the good.

REFLECTION QUESTIONS

- Describe a time as a leader when you used communication to inspire your followers.

- How do you lead by just being your true self?

- Can you recall using humor to get your message of good across. What happened?

11
WORKING COLLABORATIVELY

What would a cheerleader be without a team and a crowd? Can you imagine one cheerleader doing cheers in an empty gym (when she wasn't just practicing)? No, a cheerleader needs a group to be effective. And the members of the group have various roles. The basketball team's mission is to play well and hopefully win the game; the fans' role is to cheer their team to victory; and the cheerleading squad's role is to instill the energy into the fans and the team to fulfill their goals. All the members of this group depend on each other, because they know they can't do it alone.

"Ron, Ron, he's our man, if he can't do it, Charlie can.

Charlie, Charlie, he's our man, if he can't do it, Denny can.

(etc. with names of starting line-up))

It was July 4, 2014. Six FSPAs gathered to celebrate the holiday by playing games, sharing a meal, and engaging in great conversation. The topic turned to homelessness. As a congregation, we were already providing meals and volunteers for the La Crosse Warming Center, which provides overnight shelter to those who are homeless during the frigid Wisconsin winters. But one of the sisters mused aloud, "I wish we could do more for them." When pressed, she mentioned the need for laundry and bathing facilities and a place to gather during the day. This need seemed to strike a chord with all of us. By the end of the afternoon, half of the group present had committed to moving this proposal forward.

But we didn't do it alone. Actually, we FSPA never do anything alone anymore. The first thing we did was pray, as we always do, both individually and communally. Then we scheduled a meeting, inviting sisters **and** affiliates, where we presented the needs and assessed the interest in pursuing a solution. The interest was high. Long story short, after the initial organizing, we invited other individuals and organizations who dealt with the homeless population to the table. Many of these groups had never really talked with each other before. They just needed an invitation. And invite them we did. Together we created a movement to address homelessness in La Crosse which continued to gather momentum, and which goes on to this day.

> *"I organized a neighborhood cleanup."* (Geraldo)

Teamwork and collaboration are essential elements in a leader's repertoire, especially a *cheer leader*. In my own leadership journey, when as the president I was feeling particularly alone and stressed, knowing that in the end the buck stopped with me, God had a way of pulling me up short. I heard my inner voice say, "Don't you see what's happening? You are straying from the path. You are failing to recognize that you are never alone. You have team members, sisters, and friends who can collaborate with you. All you have to do is reach out." I got the message. And as I reached out to others, I felt the burden ease. All of a sudden my ministry as president became an exciting collaborative venture once again.

This need for more inclusive leadership and support played out in a larger arena when our FSPA leadership team recognized the need to embrace our employees as true partners in mission. This was quite an awakening for us. As a congregation, we had always been quite self-sufficient. Our FSPA membership numbers ballooned during the 1950s and 1960s to a high of over 1,100 sisters. Consequently, we always had enough people to do what was needed to carry out our mission. But as our numbers dropped and Vatican II emphasized the role of the laity, we adapted. Rather than scale back or abandon our mission, we hired lay employees. However, we sisters still felt in charge. But as the number of sisters declined and the number of lay employees grew, we gradually came to understand that the mission is not just our mission. It is God's mission. The difference is subtle, but very important. All of us working for this mission are partners, not just bosses and employees.

Once that revelation came clear, our leadership team knew that we needed to be explicit about it with our partners. In the past, we had assumed that our employees knew their importance in carrying out the mission, that they would somehow come by that understanding through osmosis. But we had often failed to articulate this directly to them. So, our team gathered the employees from all the FSPA centers to clearly delineate our mission and tell them how important they were to us as partners in carrying it out. Their reaction was enlightening. We heard things like this: "I recognize now that we, though serving at various centers, are all one." "For the first time I realize how my job is really a ministry of FSPA. I am not 'just' an employee." These comments reinforced for us that we need to clarify and articulate our mission to our partners so that together we can work to achieve it.

Women religious, because we pursue a common mission, live in community, share finances, discern decisions together, have always been challenged to really listen to everyone's input. It hasn't been easy, but through the years we have learned a lot about discernment, consensus, contemplative dialogue, claiming our voices, and sharing with others, all skills of good leaders. As Franciscan Pat Farrell, former president of LCWR, wrote:

> "Both LCWR and individual congregations have been learning how to gather the great diversity of persons and positions and weave the differences into a peaceful overall direction, if not consensus. Though it is a work in progress, we have been discovering how to modulate strong voices and assure that the quieter ones or the minority positions are safely received and allowed to influence group decisions. Such processes tend to proceed in peace and yield wise outcomes." (Pat Farrell, OSF, "A Tapestry of Contrasting Colors: Living with Polarization, Differences, and Impasse," in Sanders, pp. 90-91)

Contemplative practice aids this process. It involves slowing down, releasing our own agendas, and allowing ourselves to enter a space of mindfulness of our true reality, where we know we are one and where we work for the common good. We call it "awakening consciousness." This realization grounds us and provides fuel for our mission.

There are many examples of leaders who have recognized that collaboration and teamwork are important qualities of a good leader. One notable example was John Lewis, a civil rights leader and a 17-term congressman from Georgia. In his youth, Lewis became chairman of the Student Non-Violent Coordinating Committee (SNCC). The SNCC, although it became radical later, served at that time as the main channel for student commitment to civil rights during the 1960s. In an interview on CNN in 2019, Lewis said he saw "the need to create a mass movement, not just file a court case." He realized that young blacks needed to buy into the civil rights movement. Lewis tried to make the movement a bottom-up type of organization, where they tried to reach consensus, rather than have a centralized approach like other civil rights groups. And he was always on the front lines with the rest of the group. He was beaten countless times and jailed over forty times but kept going. (Zakaria, CNN, July 7, 2019)

Collaboration in a group is not always easy. It requires work. It depends on participants who have done their inner work and have a strong enough sense of self that they don't have to cling to their ideas. They are able to look to what is best for the whole. If group members do not have a strong inner core and are not able to engage diversity, "folly" can take over the group, leading to separation and fragmentation or silence and false conformity. Neither of these stances allow the true voices of the individuals to be expressed, and the group loses its power for creativity and good.

The leader needs to have a clear vision of what makes a good team, and then facilitate a process to achieve this goal.

For example, just before our leadership team took office in 2014, we purposely went away to another location for three days. We picked a space where there were no expectations and we were free to dream and vision, to be vulnerable with one another, and to try out our new relationship as a team. We hired a facilitator to help with the process. We told stories of our family upbringing and participated in other self-awareness and team-building exercises, like Myers-Briggs, the Enneagram, and the Strengths Finder assessment. Through them we learned more about our own strengths and vulnerabilities and how these traits affect the whole. Since we had an artist on our team, we painted mandalas which had a common theme but different colors which flowed into individually unique patterns. We later had them framed in an identical manner and displayed in our offices. This served as a reminder of how important our individual input would be and how the Spirit would move us together in the direction we needed to go. The whole experience was invaluable! We all remember it as one of the basic building blocks to our ability to lead our congregation well.

> "I initiated the use of the Strengths Finder instrument to help our team build capacity." (Kathryn)

But we didn't stop there. Once a year we again went away to get to know each other better, to review the past year, and to plan for the next. And every month, on the initial day of our four-day team meeting, we began with ninety minutes devoted to prayer, sharing ourselves, discussing a relevant article, and visioning. Why so long? It was important to take a significant amount of time to help us deepen our relationship with each other, focus on our mission, discuss wisdom from others, and recognize again Who is really in charge. Only then could we begin our agenda, centered, focused, and open to what was next.

This may sound idyllic, and often it is a smooth movement. However, while we are people of God, we are not angels, and sometimes someone in the group has a bad day, and their negative thoughts and feelings infect the whole group. When this happens, we sometimes just wait a day and let the mood pass. Other times we need to confront the person directly. And once in a while, we, as a group, need to recognize that that voice is from God, who wants to slow us down or steer us in a different direction.

Building a team and working in collaboration does not need to be all work. Every month, sometime during the week of our leadership team meetings, we set aside a night to have dinner together and then play a game. On those nights we laughed and laughed, especially when we answered questions like "What was your most embarrassing moment?" or "What was your nickname as a child and what was the story behind it?" We got to know each other a lot better and came away refreshed with more energy for the work ahead.

In less formal groups, like committees or planning groups, it's also important to get to know each other as people, both initially and throughout. At the beginning of a meeting, even if it takes more time, it may help to ask people to name one strength or gift they bring to the group. This facilitates everyone feeling a sense of belonging in the group.

When we combine our experiences and voices on a team, something bigger than ourselves emerges, something wise, prophetic, and good. As John Philip Newell has said: "It is through one another that we will know more of the Life that flows within us all. It is through sharing our fragments of insight that we will come to a fuller picture of the One who is at the heart of each life." (Newell, p. 20)

REFLECTION QUESTIONS

- When have you felt better as a leader because you worked with others?

- Describe challenges you have encountered as you built a team or a community. What helped you out in these situations?

- Can you remember a time when your committee or team laughed and laughed. What can you do to provide space for this to happen more often?

12

MOTIVATING MOVEMENT THROUGH QUESTIONS

"Change is inevitable. Change is constant." (Benjamin Disraeli) At this period in history, the truth of this quote has been put on steroids. Change is coming at us much faster than ever before. Just a couple of generations ago, a child's world would have resembled closely his/her parents' childhood, without much change. Now, in one generation, a child can hardly even identify with his/her parents' childhood. Such rapid change can tend to overwhelm us. But leaders need to face this change and its ramifications boldly and learn to find the opportunities opening up around them.

When I was a cheerleader, our gym was very, very small. It was basically the size of the basketball court, with one row of wooden benches around the perimeter, and a set of four-tier bleachers for the student body on the small stage at one end. We cheerleaders were squeezed on the sidelines. We weren't able to attain any kind of distance from the play action. It was literally right in our faces. Consequently, we could not only see the game, but we could feel it in our bodies. We didn't sit calmly shaking our pom-poms (like some cheerleaders seem to do today.) If we wanted something to happen, and we did, we had to do something. We were constantly active, responding to the changes that were playing out right in front of us. Over and over, we consulted each other to determine which cheer was needed at any one moment. Our specialized cheers had an impact on the game and on the fans, interjecting united, positive energy when it was needed most.

This is the kind of *cheer leaders* we need today. With the fast pace of constant change, *cheer leaders* need to embrace the reality of the moment, adapt to it, and then inspire their followers to create the world they would like to see. But, unfortunately, it's not as easy as it may sound. Societal changes are occurring so fast that nobody can keep up with them. And if no one can keep up all the time, we can't rely on others for the right answers. In fact, as the authors of *The Power of Collective Wisdom and the Trap of Collective Folly* assert:

> "The problems we face today do not have 'right answers.' Our most pressing problems are characterized by unprecedented levels of complexity and interdependence, and the consequent breakdown of the conventional problem-solving paradigm.... [W]e sense that the major challenges we face will not be solved by a few more smart people or technological magic bullets." (Briskin, Erickson, Ott, Callanan – pp. ix-x)

So, what do we do? First of all, in a world of constant change, it is important to claim what grounds us. What did our founders believe and do? What has been long-standing tradition? Is there something in our history that would help us in our situation today? As cheerleaders in a fast-moving intense game, we tapped into time-tested cheers that the fans knew well and had worked in the past to motivate the team.

"We can do this, yes, we can,

We did it before and we can do it again!"

Actually, questions themselves have an innate quality that draw us forward. Just as we cheerleaders asked each other about the most appropriate cheer, *cheer leaders* today must constantly pose new questions to themselves and to the world.

- What is going on?
- What response would be most helpful?
- Who is affected?
- What will ignite positive energy in us and in the world right now?

As M. Basil Pennington says in his book *Living in the Questions*, "It is good to live in the questions. A pat answer is closed, it is finished; that's it. It goes nowhere and leaves little room for hope. A question, the mystery, opens the space for us. It is full of possibility. It gives hope of life and ever more abundant life." (Pennington, p. 2)

Appreciative Inquiry (which I referenced in chapter 3) is based on the premise that asking the right kind of questions can lead to positive change. One of the assumptions of this practice is "what we focus on becomes our reality." If we focus on questions about what is wrong with the organization or person, what we will get will be more emphasis on the problems. When we ask, "What is going right in this organization?" with an appreciative eye, people will sit up a little straighter with more energy and hope for the future. The goal of the question is to highlight for the group how they can do more of the good that already exists.

Here are some sample questions that any of us could use as we do the work of a *cheer leader*:

- What do you value most about yourself, your work, or your organization?
- Who have inspired you recently?
- What do you love to do? If I were to wave a magic wand and make it possible for you to do more of that, describe what that would look like.
- (with children) What nice thing did you do for someone today?

As Sue Annis Hammond says, "Asking questions from an appreciative point of view, I still get the information I need but the difference is, the organization has the confirmed knowledge, confidence, and inspiration that they did well, and will continue to do well with a heightened awareness of what works." (Hammond, p. 9)

> "In his job review, I asked my employee where he saw his greatest gifts and how those could be better used to help our company."
> (Peter)

We *cheer leaders* depend on each other to help us find the way forward in the dark. Each of us has a unique vantage point. When we each share our deep question or insight and listen to others, we have a fuller picture of how we are to proceed. A vibrant group like this is made up of "leaders in every chair" who bring their own gifts and talents and aren't afraid to challenge the old ways by asking questions. As a matter of fact, movements are kept vital by people in the group challenging "the way things have always been done."

Beware of leaders who make it all about themselves, who claim to have all the answers! They make this claim because they may well be afraid – afraid of the loss of power, afraid of the darkness that comes with not having the answer, afraid of what their followers will say. But, as Barbara Fiand, SNDdeN, in *Wrestling With God* states: "Questions teach us ... that there is strength in vulnerability, and wisdom in not proclaiming the answer if its time has not yet come." Imagine a wise leader, in answer to a question, replying, "I don't know that answer, but I have some ideas, and probably so do you. With your help, we'll find the way forward together." How revolutionary that would be in a society where we've devolved into ridiculing leaders who don't have all the answers immediately!

A leader must be willing to lead the movement into the unknown, regardless of his or her fear and the trepidation of the group members. *Cheer leaders* must propose questions that raise new possibilities for the members. For example, our team asked questions like these at our Community Days: Where in your life have you noticed new sparks of energy? What question asked in our collective past gives you hope for the future? At the same time, we assured the members that together we would explore the answers by listening, really listening, to the insights of all the members. Collectively the group was able to move through the fog.

Kevin Kruse states, "Innovation requires a lot of failure." (Kruse, p. 168) After each failure, hopefully, one should learn from it and try again. Any movement forward involves some trial and error. But asking the question "what if?" is the only way to venture into something new. Good leadership requires a vulnerability to share missteps, but to keep asking the "what if?" question of the group.

As a leader, questions can be exhausting and uncomfortable. It's difficult to keep opening oneself to the unknown. We don't know where it will lead. There is huge risk involved. But the resulting richness and creativity make it all worth it. As Donna Markova reflected, "Questions can be dangerous. They can take us right to the edge of what is known and comfortable. They can require tremendous courage to ask because we know that new questions can lead to new ways of perceiving."

Believe me, sometimes it would have been much easier to state unilaterally as a leader, "This is what we're going to do!" without input, without mystery, without the fog of not knowing where we are going. In emergencies, of course, this method of decision making is appropriate and necessary. But in most cases, when we want buy-in from the group, everyone needs to be involved and have their voices heard. This makes us all stronger.

> *"At a meeting where everyone was stuck, I asked this: 'What is already working in our organization and how can we do more of it?'"* (Shirley)

Dealing with change, uncertainty, and questions is something all leaders are asked to do. And if we do it with humility, rely on other people to contribute their wisdom and their wonderings, and trust in the Spirit's lead, we can make a creative positive difference in the world. Mother Teresa said this: "I alone cannot change the world, but I can cast a stone across the waters to create many ripples."

REFLECTION QUESTIONS

- Think of a time when a question led you forward. What happened and what did it feel like?
- As a leader, how do you make sure that you are hearing other voices and not just your own?
- Have you ever experienced a time when questions and uncertainty endured for a long time? What did you do to see this as a time of growth and creativity, rather than just a depressing time?

13

MOVING THROUGH FEAR AND LOSS

~~~~

"Nothing is as painful to the human mind as a great and sudden change." (Mary Shelley, *Frankenstein*) The bottom line that reveals a true leader is the inevitable time in any group when change, fear, loss, misunderstanding, division, or defeat threaten to derail the forward movement of the group's mission. Resulting feelings of rage, despair, or apathy flood the members. At times like these, the designated leader is faced with a critical choice. Either give in to one's own helplessness and rage and incite the crowd even more, or channel that anger and energy by reminding the group what they stand for and challenging them to stay focused on the mission even in the midst of loss and pain. Do we react or do we respond? What the leader decides at this crucial moment will define the movement from then on.

As a cheerleader, I faced this choice often. When a basketball game was on the line, emotions were running high, and the team wasn't playing their best, the crowd could get into berating the other team's players or the refs. I may have felt the same way, but as a cheerleader I knew I had to act for the common good, to be the "adult in the room," so to speak, if I didn't want to see an ugly situation get worse. Our cheerleading squad would channel the intense energy already present in the crowd into a cheer **for** the team, putting the focus back on the mission (to win the game), and encouraging the players to play their best.

"That's okay, that's all right,

Hang in there, and fight, fight, fight!"

In this way, we were true leaders.

We all carry individual grief, but I think it goes much deeper. We carry the grief of a world where violence faces us every day in the news, where our institutions are no longer able to function adequately, where climate change continues to wreak havoc on our planet. We are in the midst of experiencing grief and loss in catastrophic proportions. Our very existence is being threatened. Nothing has brought this reality home to us like the recent COVID-19 pandemic. Now people all over the planet don't just read about the threats facing us; now everyone has a visceral memory of the terror and anxiety involved. Many people feel helpless; I feel helpless. When people feel loss of control, they can let their fear and anxiety overwhelm them. Some may try to blame others in a bid to regain some control.

This is the time when people must step up. It takes skilled leaders to negotiate these deep waters, especially since our American culture often denies death, loss, and grief. Walter Brueggemann, in his book *Reality, Grief, Hope: Three Urgent Prophetic Tasks*, states: "The prophetic task, amid a culture of denial, is to embrace, model and practice grief, in order that the real losses in our lives can be acknowledged." (p. 79) He urges us to cry in lamentation about all we've lost, because lamentation entered into well leads to relinquishment. Lamentation involves telling the truth about what we've experienced, breaking the silence so we can deal with our losses. Then, according to Brueggemann, "Honest lament... knows that relinquishment positions us to receive ... yet again." (p. 88)

On August 19, 2019, one hundred Icelanders gathered on the top of a volcano for a funeral. This was no ordinary funeral; it was a funeral for a glacier. The cause of death was climate change. This most probably won't be the only glacier death for these Icelanders. Scientists predict that Iceland will be glacier-free in 200 years. These people were crying in lament and mourning what they have lost. Their hope is that this will lead to embracing new life. The plaque they installed at the site reads: "This monument is to acknowledge that we know what is happening and what needs to be done. Only you know if we did it."

> "I volunteer at a suicide hotline." (Cindy)

Addressing loss and grief in a healthy manner involves sharing it with others. This may involve listening to the story of the loss, crying with the people, and holding a public vigil. When a leader can be with the people in the midst of their grief, they as a group are invited to join in solidarity and move toward hope. Remember when President Obama sang "Amazing Grace" at the funeral of the senior pastor of the Charleston church shooting in 2015? He was quoted as telling his staff, "I think if I sing, the church will sing with me." And they did.

Martin Luther King's "I Have a Dream" speech from 1963

is a powerful example of this way to deal with loss. In the midst of riots and beatings and rampant violence against his people, Dr. King did not rouse his followers to retaliation. Instead he reminded them of the vision, mission, and hope of their movement.

> "... I am not unmindful that some of you have come here out of great trials and tribulations. Some of you have come fresh from narrow jail cells. Some of you have come from areas where your quest for freedom left you battered by the storms of persecution and staggered by the winds of police brutality....
>
> I say to you today, my friends, even though we face the difficulties of today and tomorrow, I still have a dream. It is a dream deeply rooted in the American dream. I have a dream that one day this nation will rise up, live out the true meaning of its creed: 'We hold these truths to be self-evident, that all men are created equal.'"

Closer to home, my sisters and I carry the grief of a community which is changing drastically before our eyes. We are losing so many sisters who have been a significant part of our lives and our community for a long time. For example, in one month we buried four of our members. At the same time, we are facing a disorienting shift in understanding who we are meant to be as FSPA today. My call as a *cheer leader* for the community was to acknowledge and mourn our losses together with my sisters. Then I spent the bulk of my time in leadership reminding them that our congregation has been through many changes and losses in the over 170 years of its existence, and that we have come through with God's grace.

In each generation, we have left behind what no longer facilitated the mission, and set out into a new world with a new host of needs and potentialities. God has continually given us renewed life.

Other *cheer leaders* also have stepped forward to overcome loss and grief through renewed efforts at bringing hope to the world. I am reminded of Malala Yousafzai from Pakistan. At a young age she had become an advocate for girls' education in Pakistan and had gained world-wide attention by the time she was a teenager. But in 2012, a gunman inspired by the Taliban shot her in the head on her way home from school. After an excruciating recovery, Malala didn't wallow in hate and retribution. She returned to her advocacy work for girls' education (her mission), now with an expanded audience, becoming the youngest Nobel Prize laureate ever.

These *cheer leaders* seem to be superhuman. It's not easy to turn the other cheek after experiencing violence and instead lead people toward hope and goodness. Because of fear, people often lose trust in themselves as possible leaders and look to someone else to do it. This is what seems to be happening in many countries around the world today, where citizens have seemingly given up on themselves and look to strong despots to protect them, even it means losing their rights as citizens.

I was reminded that this has been a problem through the millennia when I came across a passage from the book of Samuel in the Hebrew Scripture. In the story, the elders of Israel wanted a king to rule them, rather than relying on God and their own leadership. After Samuel warned them about all the rights they would lose if a king

> "When I work with trauma survivors, I stress resiliency, their ability to carry on in the midst of difficult situations."
> (Germaine)

took over, they persisted. "There must be a king over us. We too must be like other nations, with a king to rule us and to lead us in warfare and fight our battles." (I Samuel 8: 19-20 NAB) Doesn't this sound familiar?

Being the one to stand up takes courage. I imagine that there have been times when each of you has stepped forward to be the "adult in the room." You might be quivering inside like a terrified three-year-old, but you know someone needs to take the lead, especially when it's difficult. This is the kind of leader we need right now in our world. Seth Godin had this to say about standing up no matter what:

> "Leadership is scarce because few people are willing to go through the discomfort required to lead. This scarcity makes leadership valuable.... It's uncomfortable to stand up in front of strangers. It's uncomfortable to propose an idea that might fail. It's uncomfortable to challenge the status quo. It's uncomfortable to resist the urge to settle. When you identify the discomfort, you've found the place where a leader is needed. If you're not uncomfortable in your work as a leader, it's almost certain you're not reaching your potential as a leader." (Seth Godin, p. 47)

In difficult circumstances, it's okay, and even recommended, for the leader to seek help. When we needed help for us or our community, our leadership team was not afraid to reach out for that help. We hired many consultants and facilitators through the years and encouraged members to become mentors for each other. As the congregational president, I engaged a personal counselor with whom I could talk confidentially when I had no clue where to go next. These various interventions led us beyond fear and loss to new vistas and an explosion of creativity in the group. We couldn't have done all we did just by ourselves.

The *cheer leader* is the one who can lead the group out of darkness into the light. Through compassion and an open mind and heart, a good leader can search out the meaning of loss and recognize new opportunities which are presenting themselves. When he or she can encourage the members to embrace the vision, they will feel empowered. New life can then be experienced in that moment. As Helen Keller said, "A bend in the road is not the end of the road.... Unless you fail to make the turn."

Wangari Maathai, the founder of the Green Belt Movement and the 2004 Nobel Peace Prize Laureate, urges us on, "In the course of history, there comes a time when humanity is called to shift to a new level of consciousness, to reach a higher moral ground. A time when we have to shed our fear and give hope to each other. That time is now."

REFLECTION QUESTIONS

- Have you ever experienced fear and loss in a group of which you were a part? What happened, and how was it handled?

- Describe an incident when you as a leader stepped forward to help the group move beyond fear, loss, anger, or despair. What did it cost you? How did the group respond?

- Name someone who gave you a good example of how to bring hope out of darkness. What did you learn?

14
DEVELOPING MY INNER CHEER LEADER

Cheerleading takes a lot of energy and can be exhausting. I was always glad that we had at least a few days between basketball games so that we cheerleaders could rest up for the next game. That rest included powering down and spending some time going inward to ground ourselves. After we got some rest and renewal, we spent time preparing for the next game. We practiced our cheers so that they would come easily to us when we needed them. We made sure we were in sync with each other.

One of the hardest things to do is to cheer for others when you've become depleted yourself, when it seems like all you have encountered lately has been negative, when dark days lead into more dark days. We've all been there! Cheering for your inner *cheer leader* at times like these takes all the strength and fortitude you've got. But these are the exact times when we need to be the best *cheer leaders* we can be. We need to tend to ourselves, so that our inner gifts may be employed to help others use theirs.

The most important practice for me as a *cheer leader* is to tap into the Source of Goodness every day, to engage in deep listening in the silence, and to allow myself to imbibe the grace of love, compassion, and acceptance. The word I use for this practice is "contemplation." Others talk about mindfulness or consciousness. This process involves seeing reality (who is God, who am I, who are my sisters and brothers, what is the meaning of my life, what am I being called to every day?). Even when I can't feel God's closeness, when the Divine seems far away, I receive the grace every day to light a candle, put on some meditative music, sit down in my prayer chair, and open myself as best I can to the Mystery of God. Sometimes it is only ten minutes; sometimes it is forty-five minutes. But I usually come away knowing that I am loved, that I am not alone, and that I have an important place in this world.

Another practice that really helps me cheer for myself is journaling. I don't follow a special formula. I just write down my longings, my sorrows, my joys, in a first-person dialogue with God. This helps me to focus and not get distracted by all the happenings of a day and my too active thoughts. As I write and reflect, often meaning, hope, and a path forward open up before me. Recently I re-read a section of my journal from years ago, and I was able to recognize how so-called problems had become opportunities for me over time as I pondered them with God.

I also cheer for myself by taking a walk in nature. Here I sense my oneness with God and with all the earth. Here I become aware of all the gifts I receive every day. Here I encounter a fox in the park, observe a tree losing its leaves, and feel the breeze blowing in my face, and I can say, "This is also me." I sometimes thank the trees for giving me the oxygen I need, and I, in turn, am aware that I am giving them carbon dioxide, which they need. I am able to touch into something much larger than my petty worries and problems, something that gives me peace and energy at the same time.

What does all this have to do with becoming a good leader? This quote by Captain Sully Sullenberger captures the essence:

> "If we as leaders and team members set aside some period of time every day, perhaps half an hour or an hour, to free ourselves of distractions, to open our minds, to maybe even go outside for a run during lunch and not just react to whatever is immediately in front of us from email or a text, we have the ability to tap creative reserve ... we can sometimes come up with the insights, the framing of a question in such a way that we come up with a solution we wouldn't have thought of otherwise." (Captain "Sully" Sullenberger, cited in Kruse, p. 37)

Cheer leaders require self-awareness, reflecting on who they are, how they have acted in the world, and who they are becoming as pressures mount. Margaret Wheatley adds: "Where has fear and distrust begun to influence decisions? Where have you asserted control? Was it necessary? What happened to relationships as a result? This quality of reflection isn't easy...." (Wheatley, p. 168)

> *"Every month I attend a men's support group where we can be honest with each other about our lives."*
> (Kent)

Knowing yourself requires having people with whom you can talk about difficult things, people who will be honest with you. It always made me stronger when I could receive from my sisters their support and encouragement. I knew they were in my corner and were backing me. And I also knew they would tell me if I was going off the rails. It's a wonderful gift to have people in your life like this. Some leaders today seem to need only "yes men," people who will tell them what they want to hear. Actually, what these people are being asked to do is to cheer for the false self, the part of a person which needs constant reinforcement, but not necessarily the truth. We are all poorer when this happens.

Often during my life, I've found a spiritual director and/or a counselor to accompany me on my journey. These professionals provide me as a leader the space to be totally honest, to discuss confidential material, and to gain wisdom as I talk. They mirror what I'm saying so that I can better understand what's going on within me. What am I afraid of? Is this resistance I'm encountering ego-driven? How can I be myself when I run into a conflictual situation? Through this process, I can reclaim love for myself again. I can learn to respond to others from my deep center and not react unwittingly.

Dealing with anger is a major challenge for all of us. Anger is an important emotion since it signals that a block has occurred in one's life. This realization can be very helpful in freeing oneself to be vibrant and energetic again. But anger that turns to rage and is spewed out at others can be harmful rather than helpful. Imagine a cheerleader in a game who hasn't processed her anger. It isn't a pretty picture! She will confuse or alienate the fans, embarrass the school, and dissipate what was united energy for the mission.

Cheer leaders must use the awareness of their anger to create a new way through the block. This can be accomplished by all the methods already mentioned – mindfulness, journaling, taking a walk and reflecting, or talking with someone about it. Doris Kearns Godwin, biographer and historian, noted that Abraham Lincoln and Franklin Roosevelt wrote many drafts of their speeches, especially in contentious times, to work through their anger and reach a peaceful clarity before they actually gave the talks. Their goal was uniting rather than dividing their listeners. Anger processed like this can became a force for making things right and inspiring the listeners.

Laughter is another necessary element for a *cheer leader* to stay grounded and effective. When we laugh, we release endorphins, which help us relax. When we relax and feel less threatened, we are more able to listen and learn. We can then think more creatively. During team meetings and other meetings, it's helpful to throw in a joke or two to lighten the mood or start the group off with energy. It has a way of saying, "This is serious business, but it doesn't have to overwhelm us or burden us."

During our leadership team meetings, when we seemed to reach a point of impasse, we often took a break to center ourselves and get some distance from the issue. Then we came back with renewed energy, and often new ideas emerged. At the end of meetings, I would ask everyone to take a moment to reflect on one highlight of the meeting, a place where we maybe felt uncomfortable, and what we learned for the next meeting. This practice allowed us to step back, look at the bigger picture, and allow things to settle within us. It brought peace and calm.

> *"My husband and I go on a date night every week to strengthen our marriage and have a great time."*
> (Rebecca)

Celebrating successes is a great way to cheer for yourself and to re-energize a group. Leaders are constantly faced with one dilemma after the other, and if they don't pause every now and then, this may eventually lead to burnout. *Cheer leading* for ourselves means stopping to celebrate what has gone right for us.

> We are the team,
>
> We couldn't be prouder.
>
> If you can't hear us now,
>
> We'll yell a little louder! (3x)

Associating with other positive, good people is necessary to continue being a *cheer leader*. If too many of the people in our lives are negative, it will bring us down. As a cheerleader in high school, I was privileged to be on a team with girls I really enjoyed. We had a lot of fun together, even as we worked hard. The same can be said for most of my ministries. When the group had fun together and mostly looked at the positive side of life, we had more energy and were able to continue working for our mission with enthusiasm.

These people don't have to be physically present. When I was discouraged in my leadership role, I would often pull out a book on the founding of our congregation. The women chronicled there inspired me as they courageously negotiated many obstacles. A good biography can do the same thing. Many have been written about good people who are inspirations to us all.

Gratitude is the key to cheering for ourselves as *cheer leaders*. Every day it's important to recognize what a privileged position we are in, and what great people we work with. We have been gifted by God, and when we acknowledge this, life changes for us. As William Arthur Ward states, "Gratitude can transform common days into thanksgivings, turn routine jobs into joy, and change ordinary opportunities into blessings." This stance toward life and leadership makes my work as leader seem like a dream job.

So, continue cheering for yourself. Embrace the good. Albert Einstein said, "There are only two ways to live your life. One is as though nothing is a miracle. The other is as though everything is a miracle." I choose the latter. And it makes all the difference.

REFLECTION QUESTIONS

- How do you know when to cheer for yourself?

- What do you do for yourself every week to keep yourself centered and energized?

- How do you keep yourself motivated to cheer for the good? Who helps you do this?

15

STANDING ON HOLY GROUND

All of us are standing on holy ground. Just as the fans wait with bated breath until the cheerleaders begin the cheer, so too, creation is waiting for us to unleash an eruption of good energy. That good is all around us. "Holy ground" implies "God's earth." Everyone and every creature around us is full of God. What they need is someone to cheer for them, to be in their corner, to facilitate the sharing of their gifts and talents which make the world a better place. That someone is you, and me, and everyone.

If one believes that within each of us resides a spark of the glory of God, then we can only be true to ourselves if we intentionally share that spark with the world. This will ask us to constantly cross borders, to encounter "the other" in sisterhood and brotherhood. While exciting and energizing, this constant call to leave our comfort zones is not easy and requires commitment, a belief in the oneness of all creation, and a deep trust in the gifts God has waiting for us in every graced encounter.

"Intentionally" is a key word. In today's atmosphere of huge and complex issues, where it is difficult to get anything accomplished, and when one does accomplish something, to be denigrated and ridiculed for it, many people throw up their hands and ask, "What's the use? Why should I intentionally put myself out there to lead and just become a target? It's too painful and may be useless anyway."

But in fractured times like these, it is important to remember that there is something bigger than ourselves at work. God has promised to be with us, lavishing us with the grace we need. As Barbara Brown Taylor wrote:

> "It is not up to you to feed the whole crowd, to solve the whole problem, or to fix the world. It is up to you just to share what you have got, to feed whatever big or little hunger that happens to be standing right in front of you. The rest will come. Because God is God, the rest will come. For now, for your part, how many loaves have you?" (Taylor, *Mixed Blessings*)

I am cheering for you to be the best leaders you can be. Look around. Remember, everyone is a leader, so you have plenty of partners in this mission. If any of you decide to sit this one out, to let someone else do it, to count on the experts to carry out our mission, we as a whole will be immensely poorer. And the earth and its creatures will suffer. We're counting on each other. Together we commit ourselves, a tiny band of pilgrims, united in love, on a journey of transformation, to bring God's life, love and presence to a world aching to be healed and transformed.

Leadership, in the style of a *cheer leader*, is a courageous and worthwhile undertaking. As Margaret Wheatley has said:

"It is possible, in this time of profound disruption, for leadership to be a noble profession that contributes to the common good. It is possible, as we face the fearful complexity of life-destroying problems, to experience recurring moments of grace and joy. It is possible, as leaders of organizations, communities, and families, to discover deep and abiding satisfaction in our work if we choose not to flee or withdraw from reality. It is possible to find a path of contribution and meaning if we turn our attentions away from issues beyond our control and focus on the people around us who are yearning for good leadership and engage them in work that is within reach. It is possible to use our influence and power to create *islands of sanity* in the midst of a raging destructive sea. (Margaret Wheatley, p. 4)

We are not alone. We believe that we are in larger hands than our own. So, let us go forth to be *cheer leaders* for the world.

>Clap your hands, stamp your feet!
>
>The world awaits, we can't be beat!
>
>Use your gifts, It's now or never,
>
>The world awaits our great endeavor.
>
>So band together; our team is strong.
>
>Goodness counts all day long.
>
>Don't be shy, don't be sad,
>
>Hope will conquer and make us glad.
>
>Let us lead; our call awaits,
>
>With courage and joy, open the gate.

GLOSSARY

- Affiliates (also called Associates) – lay men and women who formally commit themselves to live out the mission of a particular religious congregation.

- Franciscan – one of many branches of congregations of women and men religious who follow a particular call from God, or charism. Franciscans follow St. Francis of Assisi and St. Clare of Assisi. Franciscans value poverty, contemplation, conversion, and minority. They see goodness everywhere since every part of creation is a manifestation of God.

- Franciscan Sisters of Perpetual Adoration (FSPA) – one of many congregations in the larger Franciscan family. They were founded by German immigrants in 1849 in Milwaukee, Wisconsin. (For more information on FSPA, go to their website – fspa.org.)

- General Assembly (also called a Chapter) – the highest form of government for a religious congregation.

- Leadership Conference of Women Religious (LCWR) – the association of leaders of congregations of women religious in the United States. The conference has about 1300 members representing nearly 80 percent of the approximately 44,000 women religious in the U.S.

- Prayer Partners – lay men and women who commit to partner with us in carrying out the Perpetual Adoration ministry of FSPA. Each prayer partner volunteers to pray one hour a week in our Adoration Chapel for the needs of the world.

- Sisters (or women religious) – women in the Catholic Church who formally commit to living the Gospel of Jesus Christ. Sisters take vows to God, usually poverty, consecrated celibacy, and obedience, and live a communal lifestyle.

- Vatican II – shortened designation for the Second Vatican Council of the Catholic Church (1962-1965). At this council, the cardinals of the Church changed direction for the Church, setting it on a course of more involvement in the world.

BIBLIOGRAPHY

Baldwin, Christina and Ann Linnea, *The Circle Way: A Leader in Every Chair*. San Francisco: Berrett-Koehler Publishers, Inc., 2010.

Bourgeault, Cynthia, *The Wisdom Jesus: Transforming Heart and Mind*. Boston: Shambhala Publications, 2008.

Briskin, Alan, Sheryl Erickson, John Ott, and Tom Callanan, *The Power of Collective Wisdom and the Trap of Collective Folly*. San Francisco: Berrett-Koehler Publishers, Inc., 2009.

Brown, Brené, *Dare to Lead: Brave Work, Tough Conversations, Whole Hearts*. New York: Random House, 2018.

_____, *Daring Greatly: How the Courage to Be Vulnerable Transforms the Ways We Live, Love, Parent and Lead*. New York: Avery (an imprint of Penguin Random House), 2012.

_____, *I Thought It Was Just Me (But It Isn't)*. New York: Avery (an imprint of Penguin Random House), 2007.

Brueggemann, Walter, *Reality, Grief, Hope: Three Urgent Prophetic Tasks*. Grand Rapids, MI: Wm. B. Eerdmans Publishing Co., 2014.

Campbell, Joseph, with Bill Moyers, *The Power of Myth*. New York: Doubleday, 1988.

Chittister, Joan OSB, LCWR Presidential Address, 2006.

_____, *The Time is Now: A Call to Uncommon Courage*. New York: Convergent Books, 2019.

Fiand, Barbara SNDdeN, *Wrestling With God: Religious Life in Search of Its Soul*. New York: The Crossroad Publishing Co., 1996.

Fleischmann, Arthur and Carly Fleischman, *Carly's Voice: Breaking through Autism*. New York: Touchstone (an imprint of Simon & Schuster, Inc.), 2012.

Forward, Susan and D. Frazier, *Emotional Blackmail: When the People in Your Life Use Fear, Obligation, and Guilt to Manipulate You*. New York: HarperCollins, 1997.

Frankl, Viktor E., *Man's Search for Meaning*. Boston: Beacon Press, 1959.

Godin, Seth, *Tribes: We Need You to Lead Us*. London: Piatkus, 2008.

Hammond, Sue Annis, *The Thin Book of Appreciative Inquiry* (3rd edition). Bend, Oregon: Thin Book Publishing Co., 2013.

Hatt, Vince, "The Power of Being Vulnerable," *La Crosse Tribune*, August 23, 2019.

Hoggan, James, "Speak the Truth, But Not to Punish" in *A Matter of Spirit*. Seattle: Intercommunity Peace and Justice Center, Fall 2016.

Kruse, Kevin, *Great Leaders Have No Rules*. New York: RODALE, 2019.

Luscombe, Belinda, "Jacinda Ardern's Next Big Test," *Time* magazine, March 2-9, 2020.

McCarthy, Julie, "A Lifetime of Planting Trees on a Remote River Island: Meet India's Forest Man," aired on National Public Radio, December 26, 2017.

Nepo, Mark, *The Book of Awakening*. San Franciscso: Conari Press, 2000.

Newell, John Philip, *A New Harmony: The Spirit, the Earth, and the Human Soul*. Hymns Ancient and Modern Limited, 2012.

O'Donohue, John, *To Bless the Space Between Us: A Book of Blessings*. New York: Convergent Books, 2008.

O'Murchu, Diarmuid, MSC, *Inclusivity: A Gospel Mandate*. Maryknoll, NY: Orbis Books, 2015.

Pennington, M. Basil, *Living in the Question: Meditations in the Style of Lectio Divina*. New York: Continuum Publishing, 1999.

Pope Francis, *Laudato Si: On Care of Our Common Home*. 2015.

Prizant, Barry M., with Tom Fields-Meyer, *Uniquely Human: A Different Way of Seeing Autism*. New York: Simon and Schuster, 2015.

Rohr, Richard, OFM, *Eager to Love: The Alternative Way of St. Francis*. Cincinnati, Ohio: Franciscan Media, 2014.

_____, *The Universal Christ: How a Forgotten Reality Can Change Everything We See, Hope For, and Believe*. New York: Convergent Books, 2019.

Rolheiser, Ronald, *Sacred Fire: A Vision for a Deeper Human and Christian Maturity*. New York: Image (an imprint of Crown Publishing, a division of Penguin Random House LLC,) 2014.

Sanders, Annmarie, IHM (ed.), *However Long the Night: Making Meaning in a Time of Crisis*. Washington, D.C.: Leadership Conference of Women Religious, 2018.

Schaaf, Kathe, Kay Lindahl, Kathleen S. Hurty, and Reverend Guo Cheen (eds.), *Women, Spirituality and Transformative Leadership: Where Grace Meets Power*. Woodstock, Vermont: SkyLight Paths Publishing, 2012.

Snyder, Mary Hembrow (ed.), *Spiritual Questions for the Twenty-First Century: Essays in Honor of Joan D. Chittister*. Maryknoll, NY: Orbis Books, 2001.

Taylor, Barbara Brown, *Mixed Blessings*. Lanham, MD: Rowman & Littlefield, 1998.

Wheatley, Margaret J., *Who Do We Choose to Be?: Facing Reality, Claiming Leadership, Restoring Sanity*. Oakland: Berrett-Koehler Publishers, 2017.

Wilbers, Stephen, *Mastering the Craft of Writing*. Cincinnati, Ohio: Writer's Digest Books, 2014.

Williamson, Marianne, *Return of Love*. New York: HarperCollins Publishers, Inc., 1992.

Winter, Miriam Therese, *Paradoxology: Spirituality in a Quantum Universe*. Maryknoll, New York: Orbis Books, 2009.

Zakaria, Fareed, "How to Lead." CNN broadcast, July 7, 2019 (including interviews with Doris Kearns Goodwin, John Lewis, and Stanley McChrystal).

Zinsser, William, *On Writing Well*. New York: Harper Perennial, 2006 edition (originally published in 1976)

ACKNOWLEDGEMENTS

A great big thank you to all those who stuck with me when I told them I was writing a book on cheerleading and leadership. After an initial "huh?" and a laugh, they encouraged me and supported me throughout the process of bringing this book to birth. They came to understand the importance of cheering for others when it really matters.

Special thanks to these people:

- my religious community, the Franciscan Sisters of Perpetual Adoration (FSPA), who recognized this book as part of our mission to the world;
- my immediate family members – Leon Lueck and Jean Oberbroeckling, David and Ann Lueck, Janet Lueck, and Ann and Russ Knepper – who saw me through some rough patches, and were always there for me;
- my other friends (you know who you are), who kept asking about the book and making me feel special, as always;
- Mary Nilsen, my intrepid writing coach, who first urged me to use the cheerleader image as a strong metaphor throughout;

- my long-term readers – Jane Comeau, Mary Ellen Dunford, and Ann Knepper – who read each iteration of the book, and kept encouraging me to make it even better. I couldn't have done it without you;
- the others I asked to read the manuscript along the way – Joann Gehling, FSPA; Helen Elsbernd, FSPA; Eileen McKenzie, FSPA; Antona Schedlo, FSPA; Steve Spilde; and Mike Tighe – who gave me insightful and challenging feedback, and cheered me on;
- Chris, Evan, Sydney and the rest of the staff at Jules Coffee Shop in La Crosse, who provided an inspirational place for my writing and who kept me sated with the best coffee and chocolate raspberry scones I've ever tasted;
- fellow cheerleaders I encountered along the way, who brightened up and stood a little taller as we reminisced about our cheerleading days;
- the Outskirts Press staff who helped me bring my book into the light of day;
- all who have inspired me by highlighting the good they encounter all around them and participating in a "Revolution of Goodness."

CPSIA information can be obtained
at www.ICGtesting.com
Printed in the USA
FSHW010336051220
76461FS

9 781977 232724